THE SOCIAL VENTURE

values-driven business

HOW TO CHANGE THE WORLD, MAKE MONEY, AND HAVE FUN

Ben Cohen
Mal Warwick

BK·

BERRETT-KOEHLER PUBLISHERS, INC.
San Francisco

Berrett-Koehler Publishers, Inc.
235 Montgomery Street, Suite 650
San Francisco, CA 94104-2916
Tel: (415) 288-0260   Fax: (415) 362-2512   www.bkconnection.com

Ordering Information
Quantity sales. Special discounts are available on quantity purchases by corporations, associations, and others. For details, contact the "Special Sales Department" at the Berrett-Koehler address above.
Individual sales. Berrett-Koehler publications are available through most bookstores. They can also be ordered directly from Berrett-Koehler: Tel: (800) 929-2929; Fax: (802) 864-7626; http://www.bkconnection.com
Orders for college textbook/course adoption use. Please contact Berrett-Koehler: Tel: (800) 929-2929; Fax: (802) 864-7626.
Orders by U.S. trade bookstores and wholesalers. Please contact Publishers Group West, 1700 Fourth Street, Berkeley, CA 94710. Tel: (510) 528-1444; Fax (510) 528-3444.

Berrett-Koehler and the BK logo are registered trademarks of Berrett-Koehler Publishers, Inc.

Printed in the United States of America

Berrett-Koehler books are printed on long-lasting acid-free paper. When it is available, we choose paper that has been manufactured by environmentally responsible processes. These may include using trees grown in sustainable forests, incorporating recycled paper, minimizing chlorine in bleaching, or recycling the energy produced at the paper mill.

Library of Congress Cataloging-in-Publication Data
Cohen, Ben (Ben R.)
  Values-driven business : how to change the world, make money, and have fun / by Ben Cohen and Mal Warwick.
    p. cm. — (The Social venture network series)
  Includes index.
  ISBN-10: 1-57675-358-1 ISBN-13: 978-1-57675-358-3
  1. Social responsibility of business. 2. Industrial
management—Social aspects. I. Warwick, Mal. II. Title. III. Series.
HD60.C55 2005
658.4'08—dc22   2005055861

FIRST EDITION
11 10 09 08 07 06   10 9 8 7 6 5 4 3 2 1

Cover design: Leslie Waltzer, Crowfoot Design
Cover photograph by Megan Maloy/Getty Images
Interior design and composition by Beverly Butterfield, Girl of the West Productions
Editing: PeopleSpeak
Indexing: Rachel Rice

124097

To the members of
Social Venture Network,
who are changing the world
365 days a year

Contents

Letter from the Editor of the Social Venture Network Series

Like the concept of business itself—or, for that matter, like the idea of money—values-driven business has many parents. No one can be credited with "inventing" the idea. No copyrights, patents, or trademarks apply. Globally, dozens, perhaps hundreds, of organizations actively promote the concept in their own ways. However, one of the first and most fertile of those organizations is Social Venture Network (http://www.svn.org). I am cowriting this book on behalf of SVN, which I have the privilege to serve now as chair of its board. Coincidentally, I'm also serving as editor of a whole series of books written by members of Social Venture Network. I just happen to be coauthoring the first book in the series.

Since its inception in 1987, Social Venture Network has provided a relaxed and supportive meeting ground for some of the business world's most innovative and resourceful leaders. Some of their names—Ben Cohen, Anita Roddick, Gary Hirshberg—may be familiar to you. Most of the others have lower public profiles. All of us share a passion to work for a just and sustainable world. The result, with remarkable regularity, has been the emergence of new and often equally influential organizations launched by SVN members in an effort to fulfill the network's longtime mission: "to change the way the world does business." Among those spin-offs were

- Investors' Circle, which has helped to advance the concept of socially responsible investing (now accounting for an estimated $2.1 trillion, or more than 10 percent of the invested capital under professional management in the United States)

- Business for Social Responsibility which has proselytized for corporate social responsibility among the Fortune 500, with members that now include the likes of Exxon, Ford, General Electric, and Cisco Systems

- Net Impact (originally Students for Responsible Business), which engages over 11,000 MBA students and recent alumni through over one hundred chapters at business schools and in cities around the country

- BALLE (Business Alliance for Local Living Economies), a nationwide network of local businesses in twenty-one cities and states throughout the United States and Canada that have come together to celebrate the value of local business and to support one another

This book represents one more effort by Social Venture Network to promote the concept of values-driven business and to make it accessible to thousands more companies. But don't get the impression that everyone in SVN subscribes to the point of view advanced between these covers. In fact, you can bet that a whole lot of what Ben Cohen and I have written in the book that follows would provoke lively debate when SVN members gather in one of our semiannual conferences. So if you've got a beef with something you read in these pages, you'll have to blame the authors and the editor (yours truly). The perspective laid out here represents just one of many currents of thought within SVN. The field of socially responsible business is, after all, dynamic and evolving. As more and more companies begin to embed their values in their day-to-day business decisions, the field becomes ever richer in its diversity.

We're not writing these books for just anybody, though. And we're certainly not writing for the Fortune 500.

The United States has more than 5 million businesses with employees. Only about one-half of the U.S. workforce of 110 million is employed by the 17,000 companies with 500 workers or more—companies that are usually defined as "large." And, just to drive the point home, reflect for a moment on how many companies are in the Fortune 500.

Why, then, do most business books and business management courses address the challenges of running large companies? Most businesspeople work in small ones. Books about business policies and practices at the Fortune 500 are rarely of use or interest to the overwhelming majority of business owners and managers.

Of course, many books in print counsel those who run smaller companies on a wide range of practical business topics, from finance and marketing to production and personnel. But the more specialized literature on the increasingly high-profile topic of "corporate social responsibility" (or CSR)—what I prefer to call "values-driven business"—deals almost exclusively with the concerns of large corporations. (Just go online to Google or Amazon.com if you don't believe me.) No information is widely available about the special value—and special challenges—of socially responsible business practices for the entrepreneur or the owner or manager of a small or midsized company.

Values-Driven Business: How to Change the World, Make Money, and Have Fun seeks to start the process of filling that gap.

In this book, and those that will follow it, we're focusing on small and midsized businesses. Choose your own definition for a company that fits that description, but know that what I have in mind is one in which actions taken by every individual employee have the potential to affect the enterprise as a whole.

I am honored to be joined in this first book in the Social Venture Network series by Ben Cohen, who virtually personifies the concept of values-driven business.

No doubt you're familiar with Ben & Jerry's, the company Ben cofounded and led for a quarter century. During much of that time, Ben & Jerry's was recognized worldwide as one of the most full-bodied expressions of socially responsible business, and Ben was its poster boy. The company was the subject of numerous books, articles, and stories in newspapers, on the radio, on television, and online. Ben & Jerry's pioneered new frontiers in business, demonstrating—to a world that was sometimes disdainful—that a company dedicated to the triple bottom line of people, planet, and profits could thrive. Ben & Jerry's proved that a socially responsible company true to its founders' values could prosper not despite those values but because of them. The company lived its values through its choice of ingredients, its partnerships with suppliers, its exceptional treatment of its employees, and its unusually generous relationships with all of its communities—local, national, and international—and with the many nonprofit organizations it supported so liberally.

Like Ben's, my experience in business dates to the 1970s but in a wholly different field and on a far smaller scale. Mal Warwick & Associates is a consulting firm that serves nonprofit organizations by providing strategic, creative, production, and management services to assist their fund-raising efforts. The firm specializes in working with individual donors, primarily through direct mail. During the twenty-five years that I ran the company, I also founded or cofounded several other firms that provided complementary services in data processing, telephone fundraising, and online fund-raising and marketing.

During our first fifteen years or so, Mal Warwick & Associates sought to change the world principally through the careful way we chose our clients and through the support we provided them by helping them raise lots of money. Later, after I had joined Social Venture Network and learned from Ben and other leaders in the field what socially responsible business could accomplish, I worked with my board to institute an extensive program of new policies and practices to improve the ways we dealt with all our stakeholders—not just our clients but our employees, our vendors, the community where we're based, and the environment.

Ben & Jerry's started small, of course, but became a sizable enterprise over the years, achieving annual sales of $270 million and employing a total of 700 before Ben and Jerry were forced to sell the company to Unilever in 2000. By those yardsticks, Mal Warwick & Associates started and stayed small. The company (and its sister firm, Response Management Technologies) now employs fewer than forty. Aggregate annual revenues are $15 million.

Values-Driven Business: How to Change the World, Make Money, and Have Fun sets the scene for the Social Venture Network series. Each subsequent volume will deal with one aspect of running a values-driven business or one overwhelming issue that commonly comes to the fore.

As the subtitle of this book makes clear, I believe you can change the world, make money, and have fun in business—all at the same time. *Values-Driven Business* sketches out an approach to doing business that's based on that belief. It's an approach that assumes you can live a life of purpose and fulfillment while running or working in a business. This belief is rooted in my own experience. In fact, I can cite abundant examples of remarkable individuals who are living such lives *through* business. The businesses they've started or run have served as the vehicles for their fulfillment. You'll meet some of those extraordinary people in the pages of this book. But don't be misled by the limited number of profiles in *Values-Driven Business*. There are thousands of such remarkable folks all over the United States—and thousands more all across the world.

Whatever your own circumstances, whatever your goals, I hope this book will help you find the path that's right for you. And if it serves you or your business in some practical, down-to-earth manner, as well, all the better!

MAL WARWICK
Berkeley, California
February 2006

Acknowledgments

If you think it takes a village to raise a child, try producing a book sometime. The effort is almost always a community project. The two guys whose names are on the cover of this book are responsible for everything contained in these pages. If we've screwed up, well, blame it on us. But we had a whole lot of help in the process of creating this book. We couldn't have done it alone.

Three individuals deserve very special mention:

- Johanna Vondeling, editorial director at Berrett-Koehler, whose gentle guiding hand helped shape the book and keep us on track

- Deborah Nelson, co-executive director of Social Venture Network, who offered helpful advice throughout the process, reviewed the entire manuscript, and coordinated the often complicated contacts with SVN members, the source of almost all the wisdom to be found in this book

- Marguerite Rigoglioso ("the Editing Queen"), who interviewed virtually all of the entrepreneurs whose companies are profiled between these covers and wrote the vignettes you'll find here

Several SVN members provided invaluable assistance by reviewing individual chapters and supplying their own hard-won insight and advice: Amy Hall (Eileen Fisher), Terry Gips (Alliance for Sustainability), David Mager (Bion Environmental Technologies), and Aaron Lamstein (Worldwise). And Professor

Kellie McElhaney, founding executive director of the Center for Responsible Business at the University of California's Haas School of Business, was immensely helpful in the early stages of writing this book.

But the full cast of characters in this reality play includes the nearly two dozen people who constitute Berrett-Koehler Publishers—almost all of whom helped in some crucial way to bring this book into existence and get it into your hands—and the nearly 400 other members of Social Venture Network. Only a couple of dozen SVN members are featured in these pages. But one way or another, everyone else in the network played a role, too. This book is an expression of the aspirations we all share to forge a more livable world.

Preface

Nobody owns an idea. If you doubt that, just ask the guy who invented money.

Or take the idea of business.

Business has been around in one form or another for most of the 400-some generations that humans have embarrassed themselves by setting their history down in writing. If you've somehow gotten the impression that business was invented by Henry Ford or the United States Chamber of Commerce, we'd like to offer you an opportunity to invest in a surefire scheme to drill for oil in midtown Manhattan.

In fact, not only has business been a part of the landscape for thousands of years, during most of that time it has had less to do with money than with sheer physical survival. A single-minded obsession with money in business isn't anything new. Surely there were camel traders and incense peddlers whose greed would have suited them well for Wall Street in the closing years of the last century. But they lived in a time of scarcity. Not until the twentieth century had humankind created enough wealth to eliminate mass starvation and—potentially—help all of the human race to rise above the level of sheer survival.

The spiritual heirs of those grasping camel traders in America today, the multinational corporations, straddle the globe, offering opportunities for the accumulation of wealth that put to shame the most lurid dreams of the kings of old who lusted after gold. In exercising their unprecedented power to benefit the "owners" of their companies, the managers of far too many of these bulked-up businesses have created the impression among billions of people that businesses manufacture and distribute products and provide services purely for the sake of making money.

That's no accident. That curious notion has its cheerleaders in the mainstream "business community," among "conservative" politicians, and within the fraternity of "free market" economists who have dominated their profession for the past several decades. "The business of business is business," or so it's said. More and more, though, those arguments are sounding hollow.

Surely it's obvious to the average five-year-old that business serves many functions: that business exists to provide Daddy and Mommy with jobs—and make sure they don't come home every night so angry that they kick the dog; that business is needed to make toys, sell dog food, and produce cool video games. And when that five-year-old grows up, it will become clear to her that business also has a role to play in the community and has an impact on the environment (and a responsibility to protect it). And—oh, yes—to turn a profit, too, so the stock she holds in her 401(k) will grow in value and enable her to enjoy her later years.

Any business exclusively dedicated to the pursuit of profit will defy that five-year-old's expectations. Tens of millions of such businesses exist all over the earth. Increasingly, though, businesses—including many of those multinational behemoths—are waking up to their wider responsibilities to people and the planet. Curiously, as they act on that more enlightened realization, they usually find that their profits increase, too.

Many names are in common usage today for this new approach to business. The terms by which it is frequently known are "socially responsible business" and "corporate social responsibility." Other observers have still more terms to describe the approach: "corporate citizenship," "the double bottom line" (profits on one line, everything else on another), "the triple bottom line" (people, planet, and profits), "values-led business," "the blended value proposition," "the sustainable company," and other labels. It's not a new idea at all. In fact, for centuries (if not millennia) outstanding businesses have helped to better the lot of humanity while providing a means for their owners and employees to live fulfilling lives as well as to support themselves comfortably in the style of the age. In times past, when businesses started they were all small. Their owners and employees alike lived in the neighborhood. What we might now call "socially responsible business" was just a matter of being a good neighbor. But in its modern form the idea of socially responsible business is barely a third of a century old.

We're calling this phenomenon "values-driven business." The phrase is apt because it encompasses two critical aspects of the concept—*value and values*.

- The true purpose of business is to add value—not just by transforming raw materials into goods or providing useful services but also by adding value to the lives of employees, adding value to the life of the community, and adding value for the sake of future generations by treading as lightly as possible on the planet. Adding value in the form of wealth from growing profits is part of the picture, too, but only a part.

- When people in business do their jobs in ways that are truly consistent with the fundamental human values of fairness, compassion, respect, and reverence for nature, the result is to relegate the profit motive to its proper place—as one, but only one, consideration in guiding business decisions.

In political circles and in the news media in the United States today, a debate is raging about the role of "values" in the public arena. Much of the time those values are taken to be religious in nature. Certainly, many values are rooted in spiritual or religious beliefs. But we're writing about values in a much broader sense. For example, *fairness* is a value that doesn't necessarily have any direct connection to religion or spirituality (even though some people may arrive at it along such a path). So are *quality* and *democracy* and *self-fulfillment.*

Obviously, people might (and do) bring other values into the workplace that would achieve different ends, for example, the values that somehow lead to traits such as greed, cruelty, intolerance, authoritarianism, and indifference about the future our children and our children's children will face. Lots of negative values exist but those aren't our values. We sincerely doubt they're your values, either. They're not the values that animate a large and growing number of entrepreneurs and business executives all over the world who are pioneering a more thoughtful way of doing business.

Traditional for-profit businesses—C corporations, S corporations, limited liability companies, and partnerships—are just one option for anyone who seeks to make the world a better place through business. Cooperatives, worker-owned companies, enterprises with local ownership stipulations, and nonprofits offer alternatives. Each brings its own distinct advantages and drawbacks. These options may be worth considering if you're just starting out or if you're considering a strategic restructuring to reflect your values more accurately. But this book will deal only with the more familiar for-profit companies—although most of the policies and practices described here are fully applicable to enterprises of any sort, including nonprofits!

Values-driven business isn't the answer to all the world's ills. But it's a start. Without question, the balance of power on the planet today lies in the hands of business. Corporations rival governments in wealth, influence, and power. Indeed, business all too often pulls the strings of government. Competing institutions—religion, the press, even the military—play subordinate roles in much of the world today. If a values-driven approach to business can begin to redirect this vast power toward more constructive ends than the simple accumulation of wealth, the human race and Planet Earth will have a fighting chance.

As you might expect, there is enormous variety among values-driven companies. They embrace a broad array of values, policies, and practices. Some are simply trying to avoid the negative consequences of their operations. Others are actively seeking to change the world for the better. The range of possibilities is represented by the diagram labeled "Where Does Your Company Fit in This Picture?"

Where Does Your Company Fit in This Picture?

Companies that provide products
or services that improve the quality
of life in their communities

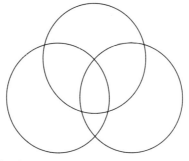

Companies that invest
the profits they earn in social
or environmental causes

Companies that are
distinguished by the
responsible way they operate

Those intersecting circles have a great deal of room for passion and innovative thinking to come to the fore. Within Social Venture Network (SVN), and among businesses that reflect similar values, numerous examples can be found within each of the circles.

- Companies owned or run by SVN members that are out to change the world through the products or services they provide include Calvert Group Funds, which screens its investments to foster positive social impact (or at least to avoid negative impact); energy-bar producer Clif Bar; Seventh Generation, a producer of nontoxic household products; natural yogurt producer Stonyfield Farm; and the personal care products company Tom's of Maine.

- Companies modeled on Newman's Own—Paul Newman's food products company, which has donated more than $150 million to charity—include the office-products distributor Give Something Back and fair-trade coffee roaster Pura Vida Coffee. Other businesses, such as Rebuild Resources, which hires and trains people with substance-abuse problems, operate solely to support their social missions.

- SVN-member businesses that seek to make the world a better place through the ways they operate include women's clothing producer Eileen Fisher; Greyston Bakery, which actively recruits and hires employees who have had difficulties finding employment in the past; Philadelphia's White Dog Cafe, which pays all employees a living wage and is a center for social action; promotional products manufacturer Vatex; and pioneer community banker ShoreBank.

But don't think for a minute that we're pigeonholing these companies. Almost all of them excel in many ways and would be squarely placed in the intersection of two or all three of the circles in the diagram above.

These are just a few of hundreds of examples to be found within Social Venture Network. A thousand flowers bloom in our garden. These companies exhibit enormous diversity. But, in its own unique way, each has adopted a broader mission than making money. Each is rigorously pursuing an agenda that includes social or environmental progress as well as profit. This is the essential reality that defines them all as values-driven businesses.

It's no accident that almost all these companies are privately held. However, exceptional publicly owned companies deserve equal or greater attention: Ben & Jerry's itself, for example, and Interface Carpets, a billion-dollar company that is revolutionizing the floor-covering industry. But these are exceptions that prove the rule. The reasons are easy to understand: the working assumption in the world of business today is that every company must focus above all else on making profits in the short term. The financial markets, and the systems of checks and rewards in the contemporary corporate world, exist to enforce that assumption at all times. Obviously, if you're running a small private business, you have to keep your eye on the profitability of your operation. But no one is looking over your shoulder and telling you that your profit margin must meet some Wall Street analyst's notion of a minimally acceptable level of profit in your company—or requiring that you show growth quarter after quarter. Privately held companies are—relatively speaking—insulated from that tragically narrow conception of business.

We believe that values-driven business requires attention not to profits alone but to the triple bottom line of people, planet, and profits. However, that simple three-way analysis doesn't work very well when you get down to looking at the practical steps a company might take to express its values more fully. The nitty-gritty realities of socially responsible business are better understood through the concept of "the five dimensions of values-driven business."

The five dimensions of values-driven business

Your business—any business—is defined by a set of relationships: relationships between the company and its employees, between your company and its suppliers or vendors, between your company and its customers or clients, between your company and the community or communities where you do business, and between your company and the environment. These relationships define what we call the five dimensions of values-driven business. They're shown graphically in the diagram labeled "The Five Dimensions of Values-Driven Business."

The Five Dimensions of Values-Driven Business

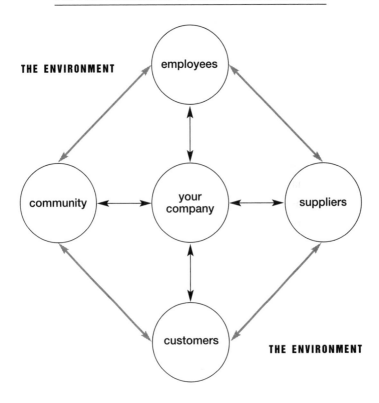

In every case, these are two-way relationships that involve giving and taking on both sides.

- First come our *employees*. They provide work, of course. But their contributions go far beyond the physical effort they exert. Their ideas, their spirit, their very presence help define the character of the business. And as their employer, we provide them with an array of inputs, both tangible (wages or salary, benefits) and intangible (support, encouragement, respect, opportunities for self-expression and for advancement). In classical economics, this relationship between employee and employer is treated as a simple exchange of labor for wages—and those wages are to be set as low as the market will allow. But these relationships involve much, much more than such a simple exchange.

- Then there are our *suppliers* or vendors, representing what's often called the "value chain." (Economists say that a business makes a profit by "adding value" to raw materials or unfinished products or by providing valuable services.) Here, too, the relationship is—or at least can be—a lot more than a simple exchange. Suppliers can provide innovative ideas, market intelligence, and feedback on our operations as well as the products or services they sell us. We can furnish them with ideas, knowledge of the market, connections for new business, and a host of other benefits as well as payment for their products or services. In the classical economic model, a business is expected to employ the cheapest available supplier that can meet specifications and not be concerned about anything else. In a values-driven business, we believe it's important to choose suppliers that offer social benefits as well as meet our needs for price, quality, and on-time delivery.

- Without *customers* or clients, there would be no business. In the traditional view, customers are simply consumers of products or services, and a company is expected to charge as much as the market will bear. The contemporary understanding of customers is far more complex. Customers make their buying decisions on the basis of a great many factors that go beyond the price and features of what a business offers on the market. The concept of branding sums up many of these factors. By studying how brands evolve, we've learned that it's critical how customers feel about our businesses and our products. Smart business leaders know that customers can be the best teachers. They can help us understand how we and our work are perceived—if only we'll talk to them. Certainly, traditional, purely profit-oriented companies are talking to them. Socially responsible companies must learn to do an even better job of communicating in the marketplace. Ideally, a values-driven business will also use every opportunity to work with its customers to effect progressive social change—through its packaging, its advertising, and its dialogue with customers.

- The *community* comprises the land and the people that surround us whether we operate in one location or in many, just in the United States or all across the globe. In almost all businesses, the employees are members of that community. In many, so are our suppliers, customers, or both. Inevitably, there is give and take in our relationships with the community. We don't just pay wages and taxes. We also influence the character of the community in ways that may be both obvious and subtle. In the best of cases, that relationship provides mutual benefit. However, a values-driven business actively seeks out opportunities to maximize these benefits for the benefit of the community. We might survey the community to identify problems that can be addressed by altering our business processes, meeting the needs of our companies and the needs of the community at the same time. In a traditional business, decisions are made on the basis of three criteria alone—cost, quality, and availability. In a values-driven business we add a fourth criterion— whether the supplier's impact on the community is positive or negative.

■ The backdrop against which we all operate is, of course, the *environment*: the air we breathe, the land and water that sustain us, the precious resources on which our prosperity is based. Even a business that operates on an entirely abstract level, producing only intellectual output, cannot survive without food, air, water, energy, and space. And, inevitably, every business leaves a footprint on the planet—often far heavier than we might imagine. Thus this relationship is also two-sided. Directly or indirectly, our companies extract resources from the environment. We also generate waste, which returns to the environment—and all businesses, like all people, are subject to the shifting moods of nature.

Those are the five dimensions of values-driven business. Some writers speak of these (or some similar group of actors) as a company's *stakeholders*. (It's a little difficult for us to envision the environment as a stakeholder since unlike some people, we don't regard the earth as a single living organism.) A business may adopt policies and practices relating to any one or all of them. We'll explore each of them briefly in this book, noting how some of America's most innovative and resourceful companies have demonstrated how you can deliver value not just to yourself and the owners of your company but to everyone else with a stake in its success.

What you'll find between these covers

The rest of this book is divided into eight chapters arranged in a logical progression we hope you'll find easy to follow. Scattered throughout the book are brief profiles that describe some of the best practices undertaken by companies affiliated with Social Venture Network. They're not necessarily either the most dramatic or the best possible examples of those practices. But they illustrate vividly the great diversity of policies and practices adopted by SVN-affiliated companies in their efforts to act on their values.

Chapter 1 asks, "So, Why Are You in Business?" We'll address there some of the pros and cons of the values-driven approach we advocate.

In chapter 2, "Are You Ready to Take the Plunge?" we'll cover the practical questions of the cost—in money, time, and emotional wear and tear—that you'll need to prepare for if you're intent on building a values-driven business. Chapter 2 will conclude with a self-assessment tool you can use to determine whether you're ready to take the plunge.

Chapters 3 through 7 deal one by one with each of the five dimensions of values-driven business. Each chapter includes a checklist of simple, down-to-earth steps you can take to act on the ideas raised in the text.

In chapter 3, "First Things First: Your Employees," we'll explore the principal issues that arise with employees in a values-driven business, focusing on those questions that matter most to employees—and to the success of your business. We'll address everything from compensation to health care, and we'll look at the importance of giving employees a piece of the action both as an incentive and as a simple matter of fairness.

Chapter 4, "Turning the Value Chain into a 'Values Chain,'" deals with the issues that arise around your company's relations with its suppliers, vendors, or contractors. We'll show you how you can extend the impact of your values through the ways you select and work with these suppliers. And we'll get you thinking about how the goods and services you buy from others may affect the lives of thousands of people you may never meet.

Chapter 5, "Developing a Dialogue with Your Customers," comes to grips with the all-important question of your relations with your customers or clients. We'll examine the marketplace implications of running a values-driven business. This will include a look at the extent to which you can—or can't—expect to transfer your values to those who buy your products or services.

Chapter 6, "Staking Out Your Place in the Community," explores some of the issues that arise when you take a fresh look at the role your business plays in the city or town where you do business as well as your country and the world—and the role the community plays in your company. We're not just going to cover the traditional question of philanthropy, though that's part of the picture; we'll also examine how you, your executives, and your employees in general can help build a more livable community.

In chapter 7, "Leaving a Lighter Footprint on the Planet," we'll look at environmental questions from a business perspective, touching on the day-to-day impact of your company's operations on energy use, pollution, global warming, and related issues. We'll show you how you may cut your costs, gain support from your community and customers, and do a good turn for the environment at the same time.

The book will conclude with chapter 8, "You Really Can Try This at Home!" If you stick with us that far, we hope we'll be able to persuade you that you've got little to lose and a whole lot to gain if you venture forth into the warm waters of values-driven business.

What's next?

Both of us ran successful companies for a quarter of a century. Our businesses were totally unrelated and completely dissimilar—one a manufacturer, the other a consulting firm. One was small, the other much larger. They were located on opposite sides of the continent and employed people to perform dramatically different tasks. One marketed to the general public, the other to nonprofit organizations. Yet, despite all these differences, we both noted time and time again that the more we walked our talk, putting our personal values into practice and providing opportunities for our employees to do so, too, the better business became. We've seen similar patterns in hundreds of other companies both inside Social Venture Network and outside.

You might well ask why so many values-driven businesses do so well by doing good. Surely the added productivity that comes from highly motivated workers and the added revenue that comes from customers attracted to your broad-minded business practices can't alone constitute a significant competitive advantage, can they? Well, in some cases they probably do. But some of the time the explanation is indirect. Some of the shrewdest minds in business management and investment research believe that the true explanation for the advantage enjoyed by socially responsible businesses lies simply in the fact that *they're better led*. The adoption of socially responsible policies and practices reflects management's deeper understanding of today's emerging social values and of the fast-evolving marketplace. Those practices are among the hallmarks of enlightened leadership.

Take your pick: whether values-driven business practices will themselves make your company more profitable or whether they simply mean you're smarter about running a business, the end effect is the same. Socially responsible business policies and practices are good for business.

Values-driven businesses have demonstrated that it's possible to run a business that makes a profit in a way that has a beneficial effect on the community. It is also possible to run a business in a traditional way that doesn't benefit the community. The choice is up to you.

Please join us now in chapter 1 as we get right down to the nub of the matter, addressing the question, "So, why are you in business?"

We've also included a resource section that lists the Web sites of the SVN-affiliated organizations mentioned in this book.

So, why are you in business?

Perhaps you run a business of your own. For years, you've been working impossible hours, neglecting family, friends, and the activities you really enjoy.

Maybe you're convinced that a business shouldn't have to treat customers and employees as expendable, ignore the needs of the community where it's located, or pollute the air and water.

Or maybe you've been working for a company that's making use of few if any of your talents. You're a cog in someone else's machine, and you don't get the respect you deserve. Yet you've plugged away, year after year.

Questions about the purpose of life and the meaning of work are certainly not unique to people in business. But they take special shape in the business world. The circumstances that so often lead people in business to wonder about life's meaning are themselves special.

For one thing, business is commonly regarded in our time as a way to pursue the accumulation of money, pure and simple. Loud voices in the business establishment, in academia, and in government insist that's so. Sometimes they go much further, asserting that making profits is the only legitimate purpose of business.

This view gained prominence in the twentieth century. In a typical business, it's now often felt that life is life and business is business. Whether you're an employee, a manager, or an owner, you're expected to draw a sharp line between the two. And if you exercise authority over others—as a supervisor, manager, executive, or owner—the prevailing logic of business implies that you must reinforce this schizophrenic mindset by requiring it of those who work for you.

Nonsense.

Living a life of purpose and fulfillment

Why does business have to be exclusively about making money? Who says so, anyway?

Why can't work be pleasant and rewarding? Why can't it be fun? Indeed, why can't we be passionate about our work, not just every once in a rare while, but most of the time?

Why can't business seek to make positive contributions to society—even if a particular decision isn't based on the least-cost solution?

Why can't employees be treated with genuine fairness and respect?

Why can't companies contribute to the health of the communities where they do business? In fact, why can't business help narrow the inequities in our economy rather than increase them?

Why can't business recognize that the resources of our planet are limited and that unending growth will lead only to catastrophe for the entire human race?

In fact, hundreds of businesses are based on the belief that a company can answer some or all of these questions in the affirmative.

Most Americans believe their lives as individuals have a spiritual dimension. When a group of people get together as a business, does that spiritual dimension simply disappear? We think not. The spiritual law of "as you give, you shall receive . . . as you sow, so shall you reap" can work just as well in business as in a person's life. Take ShoreBank, for example.

ShoreBank
The Little Bank That Could

Founded in 1973, ShoreBank is the nation's first and leading community development and environmental bank. With headquarters in Chicago, it has banking operations in Detroit, Michigan; Cleveland, Ohio; Ilawaco, Washington; and Portland, Oregon. ShoreBank invests in people and communities to create economic equity and a healthy environment. The firm considers itself a triple-bottom-line company that equally values profitability, community development, and conservation.

"Our job is to free the energies and resources of our customers," says Jean Pogge, senior vice president of mission-based deposits. Most of those customers are low-wealth members of African-American communities. The bank's home base is twenty minutes south of Chicago in a community that experienced neglect and the migration of residents and jobs in the late 1960s and early 1970s. "The area was redlined. There weren't any loans being made here at all," says Pogge. ShoreBank purchased a failing local bank in 1973 and turned it around in eighteen months.

"We've proven that when you understand particular areas and needs, you become the bank of choice," says Joel Freehling, manager of triple-bottom-line innovations at ShoreBank. "By focusing on lending to individuals, small businesses, and mission-based organizations in distressed neighborhoods, we're in a position to forge new development opportunities that catalyze positive social change and build strong, vibrant communities. They support us as we support them."

ShoreBank provides loans to those who wish to revitalize neglected houses or multifamily buildings or to build on abandoned lots. It also lends to nonprofits with capital needs, including churches, civic-oriented organizations, and neighborhood groups. "Due to the destructive nature of the racial change process in the late 1960s, the South Shore community of Chicago would probably have ended up as just another blighted neighborhood with abandoned lots if ShoreBank had not shown confidence in the future of the community by making loans to those who in the past had been denied access to credit," says Pogge. "Now it's a vibrant, mixed-income community of choice—a place where people are choosing to live and work."

Promoting conservation and environmental improvement is an integral part of ShoreBank's work, accomplished both through its intrinsic efforts to support local people in restoring neighborhoods and through the incentives it provides residents to incorporate energy-saving elements into their renovations. ShoreBank provides free energy-efficiency evaluations to help loan recipients understand how to reduce utility expenses and improve the comfort of their homes and offers an Energy Star–qualified refrigerator from Sears to those who invest in more than $2,000 worth of energy-efficiency work. "We're hoping to create converts to the energy conservation movement," says Pogge.

"For us, community development, profitability, and conservation are compatible," she adds. "We believe that trying to do all three makes us better at all of them. As we increase community development or conservation output, we make more money."

ShoreBank's Chicago branch, for example, which accounts for 95 percent of the company's assets, is a $1.8 billion institution. Since its inception, ShoreBank has infused more than $2 billion into communities across the Midwest that have helped finance the purchase and renovation of more than 49,000 afford-able housing residences and create more than 10,000 new jobs for local residents. Despite being mission-driven, ShoreBank's performance continues to exceed that of its peers among commercial banks with assets between $1 billion and $5 billion. In 2004, the bank awarded $311 million in new community development loans and $150 million in new conservation loans. That same year, the bank's losses were one-half of 1 percent. Those are exceptional figures.

The company also requires every employee to understand and implement the triple-bottom-line concept. Each person has performance goals relating to financial performance, community development, conservation, customer satisfaction, and employee satisfaction.

For example, folks who run the bank's statement processing division met their conservation goals by sending an e-mail to colleagues soliciting used cell phones and donating them to women's shelters. A customer service representative started a printer-cartridge recycling program for the entire bank. This year, with the squeeze on margins in the banking industry, employees were asked to come up with cost-saving ideas. Employees responded with an idea to cut back on paper usage.

"Anybody interested in combining the financial and social bottom lines has a long-term perspective and understands the necessity of staying the course," says Freehling. "That requires patience and diligence, and it takes more work. People have to be committed. It's harder to do business like this because markets are not set up to make it easy. For example, we were trying to decide what kind of deicer to put out in front of our building. We knew we could go to the local hardware store and buy one off the shelf, but if you are really concerned about the environment and the community, then you have to take more steps and do more research on what the most appropriate product is.

"It's important to create networks," he continues, "because a lot of these types of solutions come from trying different products. There are not a lot of places where you can go and ask, 'What did you find that worked well, was cost-effective, and was socially and environmentally friendly?'"

Pogge adds, "To be a triple-bottom-line company, you really have to make all three bottom lines equal. It's not an add-on. Corporate giving is not business. The social values have to be core to your operations. We do community development and conservation loans, and we make money doing it."

For ShoreBank, then, values came first. They still do. Wild Planet Toys exhibits the same emphasis on values in a completely different industry.

Wild Planet Toys
"The Line You Won't Cross"

Wild Planet makes innovative toys that appeal to both parents and kids. The company's products are designed to spark children's imaginations and provide positive play experiences. Wild Planet's most popular brand, Spy Gear, offers all sorts of accoutrements necessary for the budding young espionage professional, including Night Vision Goggles that feature small flashlights on the sides of an edge-lit lens (perfect for investigating the backyard after dark) and a Laser Tripwire that sounds an alarm in one's room when its invisible beams are broken by intruding younger siblings or the pesky family dog.

"What makes Wild Planet a social enterprise is how we started and the values to which we adhere," says Jennifer Chapman, chief operating officer. "Most toy companies get started when someone has an idea for a product and needs a means to bring it to market. Wild Planet did not start with a product; we instead began as a group of people with similar values, a shared vision, and the desire to develop a unique corporate culture."

The company was founded in 1993 on the principles of integrity, imagination, openness, and respect. "We had a set of ideas about how we wanted to help kids experience the world," says Chapman. "We wanted to give them toys that fostered play and imagination, respected their intelligence and creativity, and met them where they were." The company was also committed to treating workers with dignity, encouraging open and effective communication, and being involved in the community, particularly through partnerships with children.

Wild Planet reaches out to kids not only from the toy aisle but also more directly through efforts such as the company's Kid Inventor Challenge and Inventor Invasion programs. Kid Inventor Challenge is Wild Planet's way of championing children and showing that kids' opinions are important. The annual contest invites children from across the country to submit their ideas for new toys. From the thousands of entries received each year, Wild Planet chooses one hundred kids to serve as toy experts for twelve months and makes one of the top ideas into a real toy, which is then sold in stores worldwide.

The company has selected several of the resulting toys for full-scale production, such as a whimsical talking alarm clock and a playful hand strap that makes colored light beams emanate from the fingertips. "The kids receive royalties for every unit of their product sold," notes Chapman.

The Inventor Invasion project is a smaller-scale program, designed specifically for low-income and at-risk kids in Wild Planet's local community in San Francisco. Wild Planet employees host weekly invention sessions through a partnership with a local after-school center for the period of a semester. The initiative has proven successful in encouraging creativity, exercising critical thinking skills, and boosting the self-esteem of its young participants. "Our contribution of time and teaching has a lasting positive impact on the children," says Chapman.

For employees, the company encourages above all a fun workplace in which people have the opportunity to get to know one another through group activities. Workers enjoy flexible hours, generous vacations, early quitting time on Fridays, and four paid hours each month to volunteer at a local charity of their choice. "Because of the positive way we treat people, we're a sought-after employer in the toy industry," comments Chapman.

And that reputation goes around the globe. With thirty of his ninety employees in Hong Kong, company founder Danny Grossman is particularly committed to helping promote, both in-house and in the industry more broadly, the International Council of Toy Industries' code of conduct, which rallies for fair labor treatment and healthy work conditions in manufacturing facilities. "Given that all of our toys are produced in China, this is an issue about which the company is particularly passionate," says Chapman.

Wild Planet sells its toys in mass and specialty markets in more than fifty countries, which, in the United States, means its toys can be found in places such as Target and Wal-Mart. "We made a decision that we wanted our toys to be available to a broad group of kids. We didn't want to make products just for the elite," Chapman says. "My advice to any social venture is that you clarify your priorities early on and determine where the line is that you won't cross. You don't have to be perfect. Just be bold—embrace change and take chances."

Both ShoreBank and Wild Planet started small, of course. By the standards of most people in business, neither one is small any longer. So you might well be wondering whether your company could adopt similar policies and practices and still make money.

Can you make money in a values-driven business?

If you run your business in accord with your personal values, will you make money? Or will you simply drive yourself into bankruptcy in a self-indulgent attempt to do right by everyone in sight?

After all, everyone you turn to—your lawyer, your accountant, your uncle who owns a dry-cleaning shop—is probably telling you that the secrets to running a successful small business are to keep costs as low as possible and never take your eyes off the cash. They're right, of course—up to a point. And that's the point at which the principles of values-driven business depart from conventional wisdom.

Values-driven business is based on five fundamental premises:

- Employees work more productively and pay more attention to a company's profitability when they're working for something they believe in, are treated with respect, are well paid, and receive a share of the profits. They also tend to feel better if the owner or top managers aren't making out like bandits by comparison.

- Customers are more loyal and willing to forgive errors when a company's dedication to quality products and services is obvious and when they deal with highly motivated employees—especially when employees are allowed to take the initiative to apologize and make things right.

- Consumers often show a strong preference to do business with companies that demonstrate a commitment to their community and to the environment—and are sometimes disinclined to patronize those that don't. Values alignment between a company and its customers builds loyalty.

Customers are more forgiving of mistakes and less apt to buy from a competitor when its goods are on sale.

- Your business will be better prepared for the future and more likely to survive inevitable disruptions if you build stronger relationships today with your employees, your customers, your suppliers, and your community. And the planet we share will be more likely to survive the ravages of the human race if you do everything in your power to lighten your footprint on the environment. In other words, to use the contemporary jargon, your business will be more *sustainable*.

- You—as the company's owner or manager—will live a less stressful and more fulfilling life if you look at your employees, customers, suppliers, and the community as partners rather than adversaries.

No doubt you can point to many exceptions to each of these statements: highly profitable sweatshops where employees are coerced into working hard; companies that manage to sell defective products year after year; customers who return again and again to businesses with a well-known history of exploiting their employees, destroying communities, or polluting the air and water. There's no denying that today's business climate, with its single-minded focus on profits, encourages bad behavior of all sorts. Increasingly, though, companies that rush after short-term gains to the exclusion of all other considerations are having a hard time. From the biggest businesses to the smallest, they're learning that the expectations of employees, consumers, and communities alike are evolving. Business as usual doesn't work so well anymore. Of course, it's still possible to make lots of money without adopting socially responsible policies and practices. But that's becoming tougher as time goes on.

You might be wondering about those nasty articles that seem to crop up in the business press from time to time. They make the case that socially responsible business practices are misguided because they increase costs and reduce profits. The implication of many of these articles, and of their counterparts in the academic business literature, is that socially responsible businesses are *uncompetitive.*

Fortunately, the critics of socially responsible business, loud and well connected though they may be, have many counterparts on the other side of the argument. In fact, a prizewinning 2004 "meta-analysis" of fifty-two inquiries into the relationship between corporate financial performance and corporate social performance across industries found a statistically significant correlation between the two.[1] Investment advisory firms such as Innovest, a company that evaluates securities for mutual funds, pension funds, and other big investors, have reached similar conclusions in recent years.[2] Socially responsible policies and practices are good for business—and well-informed investors are waking up to this reality.

Our own experience confirms these findings. In the early days of Ben & Jerry's, Ben spent a lot of time trying to convince his board that engaging in activities that were of benefit to the community didn't detract from the company's for-profit business mission. Later, he spent a great deal of time trying to make the media understand that the socially beneficial steps the company was taking weren't just marketing activities designed to increase business. Much later, when Ben & Jerry's had become a $270 million business, there was no doubt in anybody's mind that the company's social activities drove the business and generated sales and profits. At Mal Warwick & Associates, the experience was similar. It took years for the company's stakeholders to understand that the firm's socially responsible policies and practices weren't just products of Mal's whims but integral to the success of the business.

Still, you might well be asking yourself whether any of this is really relevant to your own challenges in starting or running a small or midsized business. Theory aside, does it really make sense for you to build your business around your values?

The pros and cons of bringing your values to work

Is values-driven business the answer to all your prayers? Are you guaranteed success if you listen to your customers, share profits with your employees, support your community, respect the environment, and are nice to little children and small, furry animals?

Well, obviously, it's not as simple as that.

After all, embedding your values in your business does sometimes require additional *investment*. It may mean that you'll forego short-term profits for the sake of greater prosperity over the long haul. That's called an investment. It requires patience. It means that you have to be prepared to listen to employees you might prefer to ignore—not to mention unreasonable customers! Sometimes life may seem a whole lot easier if you close your mind, stop up your ears, throttle your conscience, and just go ahead and do whatever you please! (Of course, if you're like us, socially responsible business may be what you want to do!)

But before you pick a fight with a customer, dump toxic waste in the river, or fire an employee for mouthing off, ask yourself why you're in business in the first place. This may require that you take a deep breath and grit your teeth. But getting back to basics should do the trick. After all, you're running a values-driven business for some combination of the following ten reasons:

- You're passionately committed to your work, your customers, or both.

- You want to live a balanced life.

- You want to make your company sustainable for the long run, so it outlives you.

- You want to treat your employees as equals in a community or even a family.

- You want to build your business on a solid foundation, fostering loyalty among your customers and your employees alike.

- You believe it's wrong for business to enrich the few when so many have so little.

- You want people to enjoy their work.

- You want to share your good fortune with others.

- You want to contribute to your community in meaningful ways.

- You believe that every business must do its part to heal the environment.

Realistically speaking, every one of these ten ideals can cause trouble for you—big trouble. Check out the table entitled "No Good Deed Goes Unpunished."

After a few years in any business, values-driven or not, you inevitably reach the conclusion that every ideal represents a trade-off between what you want to do and what reality will permit. Idealism is a wonderful thing. We recommend it highly. But we know that ideals frequently have to be tempered by pragmatic considerations.

Purists may do well in some fields—the arts, for example; the sciences, too. Business is another matter. And on that practical note, let's address some of those down-to-earth questions

No Good Deed Goes Unpunished

Your ideal	What can happen
You're passionately committed to your work, your customers, or both.	Your customers may not give a hoot for your passion. Maybe they just want to get what you're selling at the lowest possible price.
You want to live a balanced life.	Reality just doesn't cooperate. To succeed in business, you've got to work your tail off. And despite your best efforts to minimize stress, everything from impossible deadlines to uncooperative employees to financial pressures gets in the way.
You want to make your company sustainable for the long run, so it outlives you.	The bills pile up, but your customers are slow to pay. Before you know it, you're worrying about surviving today—never mind tomorrow.
You want to treat your employees as equals in a community or even a family.	Many of your employees just want you to pay them well, tell them what to do, and stop blathering about how you're all one big family. They'd never marry your sister, anyway!
You want to build your business on a solid foundation, fostering loyalty among your customers and your employees alike.	The young people you hire to ensure your future don't share your views about loyalty and staff turnover. Their jobs with you are just a stepping-stone to something better. Meanwhile, your competitors are hustling your customers. You can be sure they'll be able to sweet-talk some of them into leaving you!

Your ideal	What can happen
You believe it's wrong for business to enrich the few when so many have so little.	The time comes when you want to hire a new senior staff person. But your policy of keeping a lid on top salaries backfires because that prospective new hire won't work for what you want to pay.
You want people to enjoy their work.	It starts with the basketball net and the Quiet Room. Before you know it, people are having lots of fun. But they're not getting their work done.
You want to share your good fortune with others.	Five percent, 10 percent, or even 100 percent of zero profits is all the same. It's zero. You can't spread the wealth around if there's nothing to spread.
You want to contribute to your community in meaningful ways.	It starts as a way to boost employee morale as well as to help the community. But it gets out of hand when your top managers are spending more time in voluntary service on nonprofit boards—and the rest of your staff is racking up hundreds of hours as volunteers—and far too little on the job.
You believe that every business must do its part to heal the environment.	At first, you actually saved money by reusing and recycling materials and turning to energy-saving lighting and equipment. The trouble came when the staff insisted on making your work-place an environmental show-case, which you clearly can't afford.

that may be crowding into your mind. What does it take to integrate your values into your business? How much will it cost? Can you go it alone? Are you ready for values-driven business? Those are the questions we'll grapple with in the following chapter.

2

Are you ready to take the plunge?

You've got a great business going. Your customers are happy, your employees are reasonably good at their jobs, and they like you (or at least they act as though they do). People look up to you because you're successful. The company is profitable. You may not get rich, but you and your family can afford pretty much whatever you need. So what's the problem?

Something's missing.

You and your employees are working long, long hours just to stay ahead of the game. You're not able to spend as much time with family and friends as you'd like.

Or maybe you enjoy your work, but after all these years you've started wondering what it means. If you were on your deathbed tomorrow, would you feel as though you'd really accomplished what you wanted in life?

Or perhaps you know that the world around you is in deplorable shape. You want to do something about it, and you're feeling vaguely guilty about not doing enough.

Whatever the reason, you've reached the conclusion that now's the time to do something different—to take the initiative that will turn things around, to find a meaningful way to fill that void that's been bugging you.

You're committed to make a change. If that's the case, then you've got what it takes to turn your business into a values-driven enterprise that will add depth and meaning to your life and the lives of your family, your employees, and your community.

What does it take to integrate your values into your business?

Getting started is easy. Simply sit down with your partners, or with some or all of your employees in a comfortable place far away from e-mail, telephones, and other interruptions. Take out a sheet of paper (tape butcher paper on a wall, if necessary), and start making a list of the things in life that have the greatest meaning for you. Think about the ways you and your employees affect one another and the world around you—your customers, your suppliers, your community, the environment. Discuss the quality of the relationships you have at work, not just among yourselves; if possible, include suppliers, customers, and community members in the discussion, as well. Consider what stands between you and a more fulfilling and purposeful life. List the values that you hold dearest—the values that, if truly acted on, would enable you and all your coworkers to feel that life held more meaning for you.

A discussion such as that might take an hour or two—or a week. You may be able to get smoothly through the process on your own. Or you might find it helpful to bring in an outside facilitator.

Ideally, this process will produce three deliverables:

1. *A vision statement*—that noble cause that brings meaning at the deepest level to the work you do
2. *A mission statement*—detailing the ways you seek to realize your vision

3. *A values statement*—identifying the core values that infuse your work and inspire you to do the very best job you can

With those three signposts to guide your way through the many decisions you'll have to make as time goes on, you can minimize the stumbles. (There'll be plenty along the way!) In the real world, though, few companies are quite so systematic in setting out their vision, mission, and values. In the table headlined "Thinking It Through," you'll find examples snatched from the World Wide Web of the ways that five SVN-affiliated companies have approached the challenge.

Keep in mind that the values you embed in a values-driven business must be a genuine expression of the ideas that lend meaning to your life and the lives of your employees. Otherwise, they're just words. And be sure not to pick some other company's vision, mission, and value statements. Yours must come from the heart and soul of your business—not from the Web or a book like this.

If you reach the point where you feel comfortable with the thinking you (and your coworkers) have done, then, businessperson that you are, you'll probably start thinking about what it will mean to put that mission and those values into practice.

For starters, you may wonder whether a commitment to values-driven business will mean that you're mortgaging your future for years to come.

Will this cost me an arm and a leg?

If you're raking in money hand over fist, this question may not cause you concern. Chances are, though, you'll be in the same boat as the rest of us and have to worry about such things. Here, then, are a few general considerations to keep in mind as you move ahead to implement policies and practices that will give meaning to the core values you've identified.

Thinking It Through

Business	Vision
Eileen Fisher designs, produces, and sells women's clothing through department stores and twenty-five of its own retail stores in eleven states.	To have our mission drive our business and our profitability foster our mission.
Worldwise retrieves discarded bottle caps, postindustrial stretch wrap, corrugated cardboard scrap, recycled computer parts, and more and turns them into high-quality products available through more than 25,000 of the country's largest retailers.	Worldwise is committed to the process of moving toward sustainability—living in such a way that life on earth endures, providing for our needs while maintaining the natural functions, resources, and beauty of the planet.
BetterWorld Telecom is a nationwide voice and data provider that focuses on serving businesses and other organizations that have social and sustainable missions.	
Icestone manufactures a durable surface material made from 75 percent recycled glass and concrete. It was developed over a five-year period and has a patent pending.	
Recycled Paper Printing is the country's oldest recycled-paper-only printing company.	

Mission	Values/principles
To inspire simplicity, creativity, and delight through connection and great design.	To work as a reflection of how our clothing works, simply and in connection, through individual growth and well-being; collaboration and teamwork; joyful atmosphere; and social consciousness.
To offer environmentally responsible products that work as well or better, look as good or finer, and cost the same or less as the alternatives. To educate consumers on how to make healthier, more sustainable lifestyle choices for themselves and their families.	To use nature as a model to guide our actions. To produce products that have practical purposes. To provide products that perform multiple functions. To sell products made from renewable resources.
To help organizations to change the world one phone call at a time.	To divert 3 percent of telecom revenues to organizations whose missions are social justice and sustainability. No corporate advertising.
To develop products that foster a sustainable environment.	We will strive to meet or exceed our customers' expectations, honor the balance between work and family, and work together with each other, our partners, our community, and our customers to continually improve the products and the work we do and the world we live in.
To provide an environmentally and economically sound alternative to more polluting traditional printing practices.	Print only on recycled and chlorine-free papers, oftentimes using soy, and other vegetable-based inks.

- Ongoing expenses at a values-driven business won't necessarily be any higher than they are at any traditional business. The key to success isn't to throw money at problems—it's to take a broader view of what constitutes success in the first place and to allocate the resources available to you in a way that will help you meet the demands of the triple bottom line.

- There is no such thing as a "perfect" socially responsible business. Neither one of us has ever seen such a thing—and certainly neither Ben & Jerry's nor Mal Warwick & Associates would fit that bill. Most values-driven companies adopt new policies and practices gradually, step by step, to reduce errors, keep employees fully engaged in the process, minimize financial shocks, and avoid disrupting day-to-day work. Thus, to the extent that a given new policy or practice might cost something in the short term, it's wise to proceed slowly, never getting ahead of your financial capabilities.

- As you become more deeply involved in the practice of socially responsible business, and you see the big dividends it brings, you may come to view the role of money in your company in a somewhat different way. For instance, a commitment to cut your employees in on the action through profit sharing or a stock ownership plan might no longer seem to you a "cost" but simply a way to exercise your values. Ironically, such policies, though they may "cost" you a lot, can end up earning you far more money in the long run because the business runs better.

In any case, money is not always a major factor when you seek to walk your talk. You can implement many policies and practices that will cost you little or nothing—or even save you money—as you'll see in the following chapters. Values-driven business doesn't mean throwing around money to buy goodwill from your employees, your customers, or your community. It means *working with them* to find ways that you and they can all benefit, to find ways that integrate a concern for the community into your day-to-day business activities. Socially responsible policies and practices strengthen a business when they're carefully chosen to match its core values and advance its mission.

However, at some values-driven companies, profits are the *means* to fulfill the social mission. These very special businesses exist for the sole purpose of giving away their profits. Give Something Back is one example of this type of business.

Give Something Back
Business for the Community's Sake

Give Something Back Business Products is the "Newman's Own" of the office products market. The company sells office products to businesses, government agencies, and nonprofits at competitive prices and donates its profits to nonprofit community organizations selected by the company's customers and employees.

How does the organization sustain itself? "Every successful company gives its profits away [to its stockholders], while at the same time paying their staff, their mortgage, and their other costs," points out Michael Hannigan, president and cofounder. "Profit is what's left over after everything has been paid. The difference with our company is we don't have stockholders who take the profit. We route our surplus back to the community."

To make a profit, Give Something Back must do the same thing that any other purveyors of office supplies, equipment, and furniture must do: convince businesses that the company is the best choice for their office products. It competes handily against giants such as Staples and Office Depot by offering the lowest prices. "Our business model is an effective one," explains Hannigan. "We don't have the advertising and other overhead expenses of the big national players, and we're big enough to be able to buy in sufficient volume and consequently compete with our biggest rivals."

Being socially minded does give the company an edge, though. "It helps if we can get the message across that there's also a benefit to the local community if customers buy from us," Hannigan notes. "We are a business-to-business supplier. Among our 10,000 customers are companies, government agencies, and nonprofits of all sizes and types. They all need office products and want the best deal possible. But surveys continue to show that the vast majority of decision makers would prefer—all other things being equal—to patronize companies that have a positive impact in their communities. That certainly adds to our success."

Since it was founded in 1991, Give Something Back has donated close to $4 million to a host of nonprofit organizations in the communities where it sells its office products. On average, the company presents gifts to several hundred community-serving organizations each year. In 2004, Give Something Back handed out about $450,000 in checks.

The amount granted to any given region depends on the percentage of goods that region has purchased from the company. "For example, the Sacramento, California, area accounts for about 20 percent of our business, so 20 percent of our profits goes to organizations in that area," Hannigan says.

That percentage is further distributed among organizations through a voting process. The company receives hundreds of applications from local nonprofits and then has employees choose fifty via an online poll. From there, employees and customers vote on their favorites. The amount of money each nonprofit gets corresponds with the percentage of votes it receives. "We're a fund-raising vehicle, essentially, one that reflects community needs and interests," Hannigan says.

Over the years, organizations that employees and customers have chosen have tended to shift. "Five years ago, the SPCA was the top choice in the nation. Now it's homeless shelters, food banks, and health-care centers—those places that reflect where people's concerns are," says Hannigan. "Whatever the target, we're all about enriching communities."

Perhaps giving away all your profits isn't what you had in mind. After all, the idea doesn't appeal to large numbers of people in business. For most of us, it's enough to add value through the products or services we provide and to operate in ways that are consistent with our values. Other things are extra. For example, sometimes we, too, give things away—in the form of pro bono services, free or discounted products, volunteer time, or philanthropic contributions. The act of giving may not be central to our business models, as it is at Give Something Back. It's just one of many ways we integrate our values into our businesses.

However, that statement raises an important question: *whose* values are we talking about, anyway? Are they your personal values, or do they reflect the values and aspirations of others, too?

Can you go it alone?

Admit it. As you read through our description of the process to draft a vision, a mission, and values, you were wondering whether you couldn't just save yourself a lot of trouble and do it all by yourself. After all, the very thought of getting cooped up with a bunch of your employees for a day, let alone three days or a week, is enough to give you the shivers. Why not just take a long weekend at the beach or up in the mountains and write up everything on a legal pad?

It's tempting, isn't it?

Sure, you can do that. Truth to tell, there are probably lots more businesses in which the owner or manager single-handedly sets the tone and lays out the values (implicitly or explicitly) than those where the vision, mission, and values emerge by consensus from a group. Sometimes the process even works better that way. But this approach has pitfalls. Consider this:

- If the core values you identify are truly heartfelt, you may discover that your coworkers share them more fully than you would ever have imagined.

- When employees take part in setting the terms of their jobs and the objectives they're to attain, they work with far greater satisfaction—and much more enthusiasm—than if they're simply told what to do. Thus, if shared decision making and teamwork aren't among your values, you may come up short.

- People—and that includes the people who work for you— are smart. More often than not, they'll have insights and ideas that may never have occurred to you—insights that might lead you all to uncovering hidden values at the core of your business.

Then there's the question of how you make the company's values stick. If those values are exclusively yours, if they don't take into account what motivates others among your business's stakeholders, you may find yourself swimming upstream when you try to persuade your employees to match their behavior to the company's stated values. However, even if you do a terrific job involving employees and other stakeholders in developing the company's vision, mission, and values, you'll discover that values don't magically imprint themselves on people's consciousness.

On the other hand, if your employees are a cross section of the population, you'll probably end up with values and mission statements that are very mainstream, representing the least common denominator of society's attitudes about social and environmental issues. Somehow, if you are committed to the triple bottom line, you'll have to strike a balance between the plain-vanilla values of the majority and the hearty, chunky chocolate flavor of your own values and those of your closest collaborators in the company. But whoever said business would be easy?

One of the toughest lessons people new to business need to learn is one that teachers and parents understand well: you have to repeat yourself, over and over and over again, if you want your point to stick. You need to find numerous ways—the more creative the better—to state and restate your company's values to all who will listen. You need to celebrate the actions of employees that vividly reflect the values and have a positive effect on customers, suppliers, the community, the environment, or other employees. Ben & Jerry's, for example, held all-company meetings once a month at which employees received awards— for saving the company money, for improving the quality of a product, and for enhancing the social mission. In this and other ways, Ben & Jerry's reinforced its values among its staff.

But let's assume now that your initial job is done, whether by you alone or by a mob. You have in place a vision, a mission, and a set of company values. Now we're going to step back from the picture you're painting of your dream and take a cold, hard look at the question that's probably nagging at you now.

Are you ready? Are you really prepared to cast off the shackles of doubt and plunge into the uncertain waters of socially responsible business?

Are you ready for values-driven business?
A Self-Assessment Tool

Let's face it: you're never going to be ready. To start a new business or to transform one that's been around for a year or a century, you just have to dive into the waters and do whatever you need to do to swim and not sink. Running a social enterprise—or, for that matter, almost any enterprise, for-profit or not—is close to the experience of bringing a child into the world. It's totally consuming and takes everything you've got. You can't do it part-time and get it right. So if you're one of those people who constantly struggle with self-doubt and wait until all the pieces are in place, we can't help you. But if you've gotten past that point, then it's time to take the self-test that appears in the table labeled "Are You Ready for Values-Driven Business?"

Don't get us wrong. We're not saying that every values-driven business needs to adopt every one of the policies and practices implied by the questions in this checklist. And we're certainly not saying that you have to implement all these principles at the outset. The purpose of this exercise is to help you sort through your own feelings and values to determine whether you're prepared to organize (or reorganize) your company around the sort of socially responsible ideas that have made such a big difference for so many businesses we know. You might start with just one or two of these ideas.

The question is, are you prepared to walk your talk?

If you're ready, then join us in chapter 3 as we take a close look at your employees.

Are You Ready for Values-Driven Business?

Question	Yes?
Are you willing to sit down with your employees (and perhaps other stakeholders, as well) to discuss your company's vision, mission, and values?	☐
Do you feel sufficiently confident about the quality of your products or services that you are prepared to stand behind them?	☐
Are you in compliance with all relevant federal, state, and local regulations, registration requirements, and tax laws?	☐
Are you prepared to take steps to reduce the impact of your company's operations on the environment?	☐
Are you prepared to raise employees' wages, if necessary, to bring them up to a living wage?	☐
Are you committed to sharing the burden of health-care coverage with your employees—and, if feasible, to underwrite it entirely?	☐
Are you committed to gender, ethnic, and racial diversity among your employees—and to taking steps to ensure that they feel included in your workforce?	☐
Are you prepared to screen your suppliers for environmental and labor practices and involvement in their communities—and to shift your business elsewhere if that should be necessary to conform with your company's values?	☐
Are you committed to contributing—through volunteer efforts, in-kind donations, philanthropic gifts, or some combination of these—to the betterment of the community or communities where you do business?	☐
Are you committed to sharing a portion of the profits of your business with your employees?	☐

3

First things first

YOUR EMPLOYEES

Once upon a time, when our grandfathers wore knee pants, the Industrial Revolution was in full swing. "Efficiency experts" were the superstar management consultants of the era. They worked with managers in manufacturing, wholesale, and retail businesses alike to break down the physical aspects of work into irreducible motions that (as the saying went) "any trained monkey could perform." Their ideal was to dumb down work, to make workers into true wage slaves, as interchangeable as widgets on the assembly line. Employees became commodities.

How much are employees worth?

Some of today's businesses still conduct their affairs based on this antiquated and dehumanizing ideal. However, as the twenty-first century unfolds, most of us who are privileged to live in the United States are beginning to have a different understanding of the way the world works:

- The most valuable asset any company possesses is its intellectual capital, which is the accumulated knowledge of its workforce as well as its management.

- Employees who understand and buy into the reasons for doing the tasks they're paid to do find their work more satisfying and become more productive.

- The costs of high employee turnover are often as great as or greater than the increased cost of the rising compensation that comes with seniority.

Those facts speak only to one side of the argument for generous compensation. On the other side of the ledger you'll find the hidden costs of underpaying your employees:

- Low-paying jobs attract only those who can't find better opportunities elsewhere. Too often, these are people with poor educations, limited skills, and narrow horizons.

- People who are paid too little to support themselves and their families frequently take on outside work or even second jobs, which lead to exhaustion, added health and safety costs, and increased absenteeism.

- Poorly paid employees are more prone to stealing from the company, one of the biggest roadblocks to success in small business.

- Low wages engender resentment, poor morale, poor customer service, and low productivity.

An understanding of all these facts has led some companies to reject the traditional term "employee" and instead use words such as "associate," "partner," and the like.

Whatever label they use, more and more companies are adopting business practices that make employees feel wanted and appreciated. In fact, in the face of the compelling reality we've just described, it's astonishing to us that anyone in American business today would consciously set out to offer the lowest possible wages or salaries and treat employees as though they're interchangeable. Instead—because our values lead us to consider those who work for us with respect and consideration—we believe you will prosper in the long run if you commit to paying what has come to be called a "living wage."

The $5.15 minimum wage now mandated by federal law is about $4,000 per year below the poverty level for a family of three. The "working poor" who receive this meager income impose a burden in healthcare and other social service costs on the rest of us because their employers haven't yet figured out that they, too, would benefit from paying higher wages. Because of the human costs, the social costs, and lowered productivity, a "living wage" movement has sprouted in America during the past two decades. Now, some seventy jurisdictions have enacted living-wage requirements for municipal or other government contractors. Many farsighted companies—including a number of successful businesses affiliated with Social Venture Network—have voluntarily increased compensation to match the living-wage level.

Usually, the living wage is set in comparison to the federal poverty guidelines, taking the local cost of living into account. In many jurisdictions, the living wage is the hourly rate that a full-time worker would need to earn to support a family of four at the poverty line ($8.20 an hour, or $17,690 a year at the 2000 rate still in effect at this writing). Sometimes, the living wage is set at 130 percent of the poverty level—the maximum income a family can receive and remain eligible for food stamps. The wage rates specified by living-wage ordinances range from a low of $6.25 in Milwaukee, Wisconsin, to a high of $12 in Santa Cruz, California.

Obviously, it's easier for companies in some industries to guarantee employees a living wage than it is in others. In your business, you may need to move toward a living wage in stages.

But instead of paying employees as little as you can, it makes more sense to pay them as much as you can afford. Chances are, you'll find the rewards far outweigh the costs.

For example, Ben & Jerry's sought to pay its employees as much as possible. One of the wonderful aspects of business is that it's self-disciplining. You need to make a profit. So paying your employees more than your competitors increases the pressure on you to work smarter to make a profit.

Keep in mind that it's not just what you pay your employees that's on their minds. Take our word for it—they'll also notice how much you pay yourself! Ben & Jerry's maintained a compressed salary ratio, which tied the compensation of the lowest-paid worker to that of the highest-paid worker. The ratio was five to one, so the top earner could receive no more than five times what the bottom earner was making. Later the ratio went to seven to one. Finally, it was scrapped.

However, during the time Ben & Jerry's maintained a compressed salary ratio, it was highly effective as a motivator for the company's employees. The policy sent them a message that everyone was working together and generated a tremendous amount of employee loyalty and goodwill. It broke down the wall between management and employees. Ironically, Ben & Jerry's eliminated its salary ratio in order not to put itself at a disadvantage in its first outside search for a CEO. Later it became clear that the quality of CEOs at Ben & Jerry's was roughly in inverse proportion to the amount of money they were paid.

At Mal Warwick & Associates, the ratio has consistently been around four to one. This has the effect of making everyone feel as though they're all in it together.

Try it. You'll like it. And you can be sure your employees will, too.

Wages are the greatest of all employment benefits. But a creative approach to benefits can substantially increase the level of employee satisfaction even if wages are already reasonably high. Clif Bar provides a superb example of such an experience.

Clif Bar
Building a Sustainable Business

Clif Bar is a privately owned natural foods company that makes energy and nutrition bars and snacks.

Aside from the normal benefits, such as a matching 401(k) plan and the full complement of health insurance, the Berkeley, California–based company offers "a lot of spicy stuff," says Gary Erickson, founder and co-owner. Clif Bar doesn't grant stock options—since it doesn't have stock—but it does give an annual bonus based on the company's performance as well as tax credits for child-care costs. Time is money, too, so the company also offers four weeks of vacation, flexible work hours, and "9/80" scheduling, which allows employees to work a little more time each day and then take every other Friday off. After seven years of service, staff members may take a ninety-day paid sabbatical, and an additional ninety days of unpaid leave if they want a full six-month stretch.

An on-site gym runs a variety of classes during workdays and is staffed with personal trainers. To further help reduce stress and the time employees spend running errands, the company hosts various fee-based services, including on-site haircutting, massage, laundry/dry cleaning pickup and delivery, car washing, dog walking, oil change/car service, and prepared meals from Home on the Range Catering.

Recreational activities, such as skiing, camping trips, picnics, and excursions to baseball games, help create a sense of solidarity among workers. The Epiphany Bike Ride, commemorating the ride Erickson was on when he came up with the idea for the original Clif Bar, is a special highlight.

The perks work. "We have very little voluntary turnover, less than 1 percent," says Erickson. "Many people are here for a long time because in Clif Bar they've found their sweet spot."

But it's more than just benefits that get Cliffies up in the morning—it's the whole feel of the place. "People say that when they walk in here there's a special energy that's palpable," says Erickson. "People are focused yet playful and balanced."

A lot of the credit for that goes to Erickson and his wife, Kit Crawford, owners since the birth of Clif Bar. "We don't have an exit strategy or plans to sell out to a multinational corporation," Erickson says. "We're here to stay, and there are no hidden agendas. I think our employees pick up on that and respond with loyalty."

The company's vision also appeals to Clif Bar employees. "We have five bottom lines: the planet, the community, our own people, the health of our brands, and the health of our business model. We're building a sustainable business and not just going for the big numbers, and our staff appreciates that," Erickson says.

As a part of that mission, employees are inspired to fulfill a total of 2,080 hours of community service yearly in the local San Francisco Bay Area. (Erickson explains 2,080 hours is equivalent to the work of one full-time employee in a year.) They may serve alone or in groups during regular work hours. Group activities are arranged, for example, for organizations such as Habitat for Humanity, Meals on Wheels, Ma and Pa Green, San Francisco General Hospital, AIDS Walk, and more. The company's forty-six sales and marketing staffers who reside in other states similarly serve in their local communities.

"Not only do the recipients benefit, but employees and salespeople have the satisfaction of giving back to people in need, and they have the opportunity to work with other members of our organization whom they may not normally get to know. It's been a very successful program, and we have always exceeded the 2,080-hour target," says Erickson. For the second year running, the company is also partnering with the international arm of Habitat for Humanity to send three employees abroad for two weeks (Romania last year, Poland this year) to help build houses. Clif Bar picks up all costs for the three staff members selected to go through an application process.

Erickson and his wife take care to know all of their 150 employees by name. Erickson himself chairs or shows up at the company-wide meeting every week, and his wife hosts an intimate afternoon tea once a month. "Just hanging out and talking goes a long way toward building trust, which is a big issue in any company," he says.

Erickson's advice: "Never expect that just because you have a great company, a great business model, and great employees, things are going to be perfect. You have to keep tweaking it."

An open-minded approach to benefits can go a long way to bolster employees' loyalty. Ben & Jerry's, for example, was one of the first companies to provide health insurance for domestic partners. The company also worked with a health insurance company to provide coverage for alternative medical care. At Mal Warwick & Associates, too, an unusually long list of employee benefits, including many that are rarely considered, helps make the company special and convey the message that employees really matter.

However, no matter how generous and flexible the benefits a company offers, long-tenured employees may have a tendency to wonder why they're not receiving a share of the profits—particularly if the business, like Clif Bar, Ben & Jerry's, or Mal Warwick & Associates, treats them exceptionally well.

Sharing the wealth

The base wage or salary you pay is the single most important number in your workers' minds. No manner of benefit enhancements, bonuses, profit sharing, or other supplementary means of compensation is likely to have equal impact. Still, you can go a long way toward making your employees feel like your partners when you institute some form of bonus or profit-sharing program.

You can take your pick of a number of different approaches. Among them are the following:

- A simple bonus system in which employees receive a percentage of the quarterly, semiannual, or annual pretax net income in proportion to their relative annual pay. A variation on this approach is to pay a bonus linked to seniority rather than salary level, as was the case at Ben & Jerry's, where 5 percent of pretax net was earmarked for this purpose.

- "Gain sharing," which involves performance bonuses to individual work teams proportional to their attainment of their objectives.

- A bonus system in which a percentage of the pretax net is set aside in a bonus pool in which all full-time employees share equally, regardless of compensation (and part-time employees receive equivalent proportions).

- Deferred compensation in the form of stock options offered at advantageous prices, outright grants of stock, or one of several types of retirement plan into which the company pays either a matching amount or an unconditional percentage of each employee's compensation.

- Employee ownership schemes, including the federal Employee Stock Ownership Program (ESOP), under which shares of a company's stock are transferred—suddenly or gradually—into a trust from which individual employees can draw upon leaving the company or retiring.

- A genuine employee ownership program designed to transfer voting stock to workers and give them a say in the company's strategy as well as in its profits. At Mal Warwick & Associates, an ESOP is just one of several systems in place—including sales or gifts of stock to selected "key" employees—to transfer ownership from the founder to the employees, with an ultimate goal of 100 percent employee ownership.

There's no lack of reasons why you should consider adopting some such program. Employees who fully recognize that their individual actions help determine how much money the company makes tend to work harder and more effectively. They're much more likely to take the initiative to correct errors or head off problems. They become goodwill ambassadors with customers, prospective employees, suppliers, and the community at large. They approach their work with an owner's perspective, taking responsibility or even taking the initiative when it's not explicitly required of them. That's the business case for sharing profits. But there's another reason to do so.

The gap between rich and poor in America is reflected in the enormous difference in income between them. When the average annual compensation for the twenty-five top hedge-fund managers is a quarter-billion dollars while employees at fast-food restaurants bring home barely more than $10,000, there's no mistaking the contrast. But the more meaningful contrast that brings even more far-reaching, long-term consequences is the asset gap between rich and poor: *the bottom 40 percent of the American people hold just 0.5 percent of the nation's total wealth.*

What is wealth? For most Americans, it's the equity in a residence that ensures the family will never be homeless. It's a savings account that provides a cushion in the event of a lost job or an emergency. It's a life insurance policy that will provide for surviving family members in the event of a breadwinner's untimely death. It's a personal investment account that will pay for the kids to go to college. It's a retirement plan that will supplement Social Security and allow a family's oldest members to live in dignity and a semblance of comfort. Alarming numbers of Americans today possess none of these forms of wealth.

In other words, for all intents and purposes, nearly half the U.S. population is at best only a step above destitution—just one paycheck away from catastrophe.

But those of us in business can do something about this all by ourselves. We can help pave the way for our own employees to build wealth for themselves and their families—through profit sharing and employee ownership. At Mal Warwick & Associates, these policies are among the company's most significant commitments to social responsibility.

Mal Warwick & Associates
Sharing a Piece of the Action

Each quarter, Mal Warwick & Associates transfers 35 percent of its pretax profits to a profit-sharing fund. The money in the fund is then divided in roughly equal shares among all employees. Slight variations occur from one business unit to another. Full-time data-entry specialists receive shares of approximately the same dollar amount as do the chairman and the CEO— sometimes a few dollars more. Individual bonuses vary with the number of hours worked. Even part-time employees get checks if they've worked for the company for at least three months.

The company introduced this practice to give employees a share in the fruits of their work. But profit sharing proved to be at least as big a benefit to the company as it was to the employees. The company's managers underestimated by a large margin, the dramatic lift in productivity that followed the introduction of the profit-sharing plan. For the firm's more modestly paid employees, it made the difference between living comfortably and just getting by—and that made it possible for many more employees to participate in the company's Philanthropic Fund (see chapter 6), making charitable contributions for the first time ever.

This practice was introduced—over strenuous objections from some senior managers and members of the board—strictly out of a desire to give the company's employees a meaningful stake in the company's success. It was hoped, too, that the practice would encourage employees to think more closely about how their individual actions might contribute to the firm's financial performance.

Immediately after the profit-sharing plan was instituted, the company's performance began to improve markedly. Profits, which had been very meager the preceding year, rose significantly. During the first quarter after the plan debuted, bonuses amounted to approximately $30 per employee, which occasioned a great deal of snickering. The next quarter the bonus ran about $300. That considerably reduced the snickering. When, the following quarter, the bonus rose to about $1,000, most of the employees became true believers.

During subsequent years, profits rose considerably further. Over the five-year period following the introduction of profit sharing, the company realized total profits greater than during the preceding twenty years—even when comparing results *after* deducting for profit-sharing payouts.

Other factors contributed to this dramatic improvement, of course. But the company's board concluded in an assessment of the program's impact about two years after its initiation that profit sharing had played a significant role in bolstering the company's financial bottom line.

The profit-sharing plan was adopted only after lively and protracted debate on the board. The CFO and consulting accountant, with support from other board members, argued that the earmarking of 45 percent of pretax net profits each quarter—35 percent for profit sharing and 10 percent for the Philanthropic Fund—ran the substantial risk of bankrupting the company in the event that profits were high for a time and then sharply declined. Removing that much money from retained earnings could leave the company with a troubled balance sheet. Despite these risks, the board elected to implement the program as a matter of principle. From a purely financial perspective, the dissenters were right, no doubt. But this program involved a lot more than just financial questions.

Profit sharing reflects the core values of the staff of Mal Warwick & Associates. Other companies, with an equal commitment to the triple bottom line, have found different ways to share the wealth that more closely embody their own values. Eileen Fisher is a great example.

Eileen Fisher
A Joyful Culture

Eileen Fisher Inc. designs, produces, and sells women's clothing known for being elegant yet simple and versatile. The company sports threads in all leading upscale department stores as well as in specialty stores and its own retail establishments. With 600 employees and revenues last year of $177 million, the company, headquartered north of Manhattan in Irvington, New York, is certainly large by comparison with most U.S. companies. One might therefore expect it to be plagued by the usual bureaucracy and impersonality that hit an organization once it reaches a certain critical mass. Yet for the second year in row,

Eileen Fisher has been named one of the twenty-five best medium-sized companies to work for in America by the same group that posts the Fortune 500 list. How does it manage to be both hefty and humane?

"A lot has to do with our commitment to our mission," says Susan Schor, who, as the company's chief culture officer, is just one of scores of company leaders responsible for ensuring that the Eileen Fisher philosophy is nurtured and integrated throughout the organization. The organization's overall aim is to inspire "simplicity, creativity, and delight" through the design of elegant clothing and the fostering of a collaborative, caring culture. "That philosophy applies not just to customers but to all of our employees, from the maintenance team to the designers and leaders," says Schor.

The company stresses individual growth and well-being, career/family balance, teamwork, the creation of a joyful atmosphere, and social consciousness. And the organization demonstrates its commitment to those values in a number of ways. One is by promoting a culture that eschews hierarchy and cultivates collaboration. "Our leaders aim to facilitate and not direct others," says Schor. "We think together, process together, and integrate people from a number of places across the organization in decision making. For some people, this can be frustrating because it means things take longer to accomplish and not all input gets acted upon. But we believe we end up in the best place as a result of such a process."

Another way Eileen Fisher delights its employees is by offering an elaborate benefits package, which includes full health, dental, and life insurance, twelve-week paid maternity leave for mothers, three-week paid "maternity" leave for fathers and partners, guidance with child care and elder dependent care, and the option of flexible work hours. (In fact, the head honcho herself, Eileen Fisher, quits at two-thirty in order to be with her school-age children.) Profit sharing over the last three years has amounted to a whopping six to eight weeks' worth of salary for each person, paid in a lump sum at the end of the year.

And the goodies don't stop there. The company also offers a "wellness benefit": $1,000 per calendar year for each person to spend on classes, activities, and treatments related to mind-body health. "By helping our employees to get and stay well," says the company's social consciousness director, Amy Hall, "we expect to have a happier, more productive workforce!

"Eileen, our founder and president, has long understood the benefits of complementary therapies and wanted to find ways to make them more accessible to her employees. By doing so, our hope is that employees will not only be happier, healthier, and more productive but that our cost for health insurance may ultimately decrease as a result of employees taking better care of themselves."

Fisher herself worked with the company's Human Resources Department to design the initiative. Employees turn in receipts after participating in a service or activity, and they're reimbursed in the next pay period, up to a total of $1,000 per year. An employee wellness committee reviews any services/activities that fall outside the normal list.

"We firmly believed that by encouraging employees to take care of themselves," adds Hall, "they would be healthier for it, and that would show up *somehow* on the job. The most significant observable result has been very high employee morale. Further, this particular benefit helps us in recruiting as well as in keeping employees. Indeed, while it's not directly attributable to just this wellness benefit, our retention and recruitment rates have been dramatically higher than industry averages. Almost everyone in the company makes use of it.

"Another result we hoped for was that healthier, happier employees would lead to lower health insurance costs. We don't know yet if this is the case. Still, in light of the other positive results, and because wellness is central to our company culture, we anticipate only opportunities for maintaining and/or growing the program."

The company itself already provides numerous on-site yoga classes, nutrition workshops, and reflexology and massage sessions, as well as special dance and movement activities and classes, the bulk of which are integrated into the workday in one way or another. "We frequently start our meetings with stretching and punctuate them by doing conscious breathing or chair yoga, for example," says Schor.

Then there's the additional $1,000 a year granted to each person for education, be it related to work or not. "People might take, say, a guitar or dance class or something more academic," says Schor. And perhaps the pièce de résistance for the organization's employees—85 percent of whom are women—is a generous clothing allowance for purchasing Eileen Fisher designs. "Even the men who work with us get an allowance so they can order clothing for the women in their lives," Schor says.

"For us, creating a joyful culture is not a tactic to get more out of people and make more money. It emerges from a belief system, promoted by our founder Eileen Fisher twenty years ago, that this is simply the right way to be with our people," says Schor.

Not surprisingly, hardly anyone ever quits. "Administratively, we have only a 7 percent turnover, and in our stores we have a low 12 percent. That's well below the industry standard for retail, which is close to about 50 percent," says Schor. "On surveys, 90 percent of our employees rate this as a great place to work."

In fact, with so many of their longings satisfied on numerous levels of psychologist Abraham Maslow's proverbial hierarchy of needs, Eileen Fisher employees are motivated to work—and work hard. "Sometimes our efforts are devoted to getting them to stop, to not work nights and weekends," Schor says. Now that's a problem any company would be happy to have.

In a highly profitable company such as Eileen Fisher, it's relatively easy to marshal the resources to introduce novel benefit programs to match the company's values. For your business, that may not be the case. In fact, most of us have to consider the financial limitations we face—and to weigh the trade-off between added benefits and higher pay.

How many benefits are enough?

In some sectors of the economy, employees routinely calculate the value—whether tangible or intangible—of the benefits they receive. They look on their compensation as a whole; teachers, for example, who are typically granted long summer vacations; employees at companies that provide full health insurance, which is often prohibitively expensive (or completely unobtainable) for individuals on their own; or workers at that fast-shrinking number of major corporations that still make generous annual payments into pension funds. But at most small and midsized companies, the benefits employees receive are normally limited. It can be a challenge to persuade workers that even minimal employment benefits are equivalent to 10 percent, 15 percent, or more of their total compensation. Benefits are too often taken for granted.

From your perspective, of course, you see a clear trade-off between raising pay and expanding benefits. Either way, you pay. From your employees' point of view, though, there may be a big difference between the two forms of compensation. If you take the radical step of *asking* employees for their preferences, you may be surprised. Even people in their twenties and thirties who you might think would have no inkling of the need to provide for retirement may opt for a 401(k) plan instead of a raise. That's exactly what happened at Mal Warwick & Associates and its sister company, Response Management Technologies, when management polled the staff to determine their preferences. And it's anybody's guess how employees might choose between, say, free lunches and a wellness program including yoga and weight training.

Some benefits cost little or nothing, but employees may perceive them to have high value, anyway. At Ben & Jerry's, for example, each employee was entitled to three free pints of ice cream a day—and to free massages. The cost was minimal, the impact substantial. Both benefits communicated a sense of caring, probably more than far costlier but less distinctive benefits such as the retirement plan.

At Ted Nace's Peachpit Press, one of the principal benefits that helped attract and retain great employees was an unusually generous vacation policy. "At Peachpit we allowed vacations of any length whatsoever," explains Nace, "provided the person taking an extended leave arranged for someone else on the staff to cover for them. In practice, this meant that people ended up cross-training other people and doing extended swaps (e.g., so someone could take a four-month trip or stay home for a year with a baby). So our staff, overall, became much better trained. Also, because we allowed people to undertake big travel adventures without having to quit their jobs, people stayed much longer with the company."

Whatever your company's financial circumstances, there will, of course, be a limit to how much you can afford to pay your workers. Tax considerations may enter into the picture, too. They'll understand all that. (They may not like it, but that's another story.) You will gain the maximum benefit in morale and productivity if you allow your employees to participate in choosing how to allocate the available funds. A "cafeteria plan" that provides a choice of benefits may be an excellent option for your company. Giving your employees a share of decision-making power is just one of many ways that you can maximize the return on the considerable investment you make in hiring, training, supervising, and compensating your employees.

Here are three other ways you can improve employee morale, foster loyalty, raise the quality of customer service, and have a lot of fun:

■ Appoint a popular employee (someone who's not a manager) as the company's social secretary. Give him a budget and empower him to organize a free lunch for all employees once a month. Encourage him to adopt a different theme each month, but let him and those he recruits to help him use their imaginations and procure the food wherever they choose. This is a practice recently adopted at Mal Warwick & Associates. It works.

■ Once a year, schedule a recycling day in your office. Free up as many of your employees as you possibly can to clean up and reorganize their workspaces. Urge them to identify as much paper and other recyclable material as they possibly can. Offer prizes for the employee who recycles the most, for the person who comes closest to guessing the height of the stack of paper in the office of the company's biggest pack rat, for the "best rookie" effort, and for the "most improved" since the previous year. Use your imagination to come up with other trivial contests, and hand out silly, inexpensive prizes at a staff meeting at the end of the day. This is a long-standing practice at Mal Warwick & Associates, where it's called National Discard Day.

- At least once a year, organize an open meeting of all your employees to discuss how the company might improve its performance on the social bottom line. Ask what new policies or practices you could put in place. Run the meeting as a brainstorming session. Record every suggestion, no matter how wacky. Chances are, you'll identify at least one idea that can be put into practice without great muss or fuss.

Benefits come in packages that are big, small, or in-between. For most companies, benefits are in some way optional. They're granted at the discretion of the owner or managers. Not so at Vatex America.

Vatex America
Employee Rights, Not Benefits

Vatex America was started in 1975 as a single retail T-shirt store called the Dirt Shirt. Today, it is one of the largest and most recognized screen printers and promotional products distributors in the country, providing corporate clients with anything from logo-bearing desk accessories, mugs, and towels to wearables such as hats and shirts.

"The premise of Vatex," says founder and CEO Jerry Gorde, "is that if capitalism is the ultimate economic engine and democracy is the ultimate governance process, then the two should be combined." Employees become part owners after six years with the company, during which time they must pass in-house courses on intrapreneurship and the basics of how businesses operate. After that, they gain a financial stake in the company and, as "owner-employees," a say in company policy.

"They begin empowering themselves by taking ownership of their own destinies and by seeing their destinies linked to those of others, whether it be their own families, their community, or their business," says Gorde.

At Vatex, owner-employees do not have "benefits." "'Benefits' are those things the paternalistic system has determined people are not naturally entitled to," says Gorde. Rather, they partake of "owner-employee rights," including a guaranteed living wage (set well above the industry standard), a healthy workplace; reimbursed educational expenses for professional and personal development, 80 percent of full health-care coverage, end-of-year profit sharing ("the profits are automatically everyone's," says Gorde), and commercial use of both an on-site gym and organic garden.

The equivalent of the "working class" of the company—the shop floor workers—are among the most committed to the Vatex model. "We're moving to emancipate those who have suffered because of social and economic injustices in our society," Gorde says. "Some employee-owners leave, however, because they think that having to share and align themselves with the needs of so many other people is a colossal waste of time and a distraction from earning money," Gorde acknowledges.

Jerry Gorde's approach to employee benefits at Vatex represents one values-driven perspective. Doug Hammond's at Relief Resources reveals another.

Relief Resources
Bottom-Line Benefits

Relief Resources was founded in Boston in 1979 as the first staffing agency in the country exclusively dedicated to the human services industry. The organization provides temporary, interim, and long-term staffing for behavioral health, child-care, and human services organizations, which include government agencies and departments, independent vendors of the state, and private firms. If your organization is in Massachusetts, Rhode Island, or parts of Connecticut and you need a professional—or an entire staff of professionals—in mental health, elder care, child care, or any other social service area, you're likely to find your match at Relief Resources.

Most temporary employment agencies in other fields over-stuff the ranks of their available staff by as much as 200 percent to ensure that when a call comes in they have a person to fill the position. But this leaves their workers spottily employed, says Doug Hammond, Relief Resources' president and founder. "We have a rule whereby we staff only at 110 percent so that our people can maintain sustainable employment while enjoying the flexibility that goes along with being a temp," he explains. "This allows us to develop a relationship with them that's based on honesty and inclusion." Such an approach is particularly appreciated by the kinds of people who come to join the Relief Resources team: frequently first- and second-generation immigrants who are often vulnerable to exploitation by employers. "We provide a safe pathway to those entering the industry in this country," Hammond says.

The agency also provides an atmosphere in which people can bring their whole selves through the door. "People are encouraged to let us know who they are and what's going on in their lives, what their needs are," Hammond says. The soulful model helps foster loyalty and motivation on the part of the organization's approximately 350 human services workers. "If challenges come up on the job, our people are more likely to work through them and stick with it because they know they're part of our community," Hammond says. Such an approach to employment also leads to a remarkably low turnover rate, particularly in comparison to the rest of the human services industry, which sees turnover as high as 40 to 60 percent a year for direct care work. "Our people generally stay with us three or four years—which is four to five times longer than the industry standard—and the reasons they move on are generally that they're relocating or we have placed them into something permanent," Hammond notes. "We also have an open-door policy that encourages them to come back to us when they want or need to."

Because Relief Resources has such a positive reputation as an employer, the company does not need to spend much time, energy, and money recruiting field staff. "Most of our workers come from referrals from other employees or from people in the community. That means we hardly have to do any advertising, which is the biggest expense for most temp agencies," Hammond says. "Our investment in relationships has yielded incredible bottom-line benefits in terms of cost savings, which, in turn, allows us to keep our rates more affordable for our clients."

For the administrative employees who keep the organization running, Relief Resources is similarly heart-centered and flexible. "One of our commitments is to allow for the fact that people's lives change and so do their employment needs," says Hammond. "We have folks who have wanted to reduce their hours in order to create more time to start their own businesses, go to school, or have families, and we always allow them the freedom to reduce their hours or change roles to accommodate that. Others shift their hours to help them." The new arrangement nearly always results in a boost in individuals' motivation and sense of personal joy and allows the organization to retain its institutional knowledge, he observes.

Hammond himself has also shifted over the years from being a best-practices "cheerleader" to a best-practices "supporter." "I don't try to push things on our organization anymore—like creating the perfect recycling program. I help create an atmosphere that allows people to incorporate social values at the level that works for them. The most important thing is that people feel good here and that we keep it fun." Which, in the final analysis, may be one of the most important lessons a socially responsible owner or manager can learn!

Jerry Gorde's approach at Vatex America and Doug Hammond's at Relief Resources are different, as you can clearly see. Gorde has moved aggressively to put in place an extraordinarily progressive employee-ownership program. Hammond has elected not to push so hard to imprint his own values on others. Each has found his own way to share his passion with his employees. Both ways work. They illustrate two contrasting approaches to one of the central issues in running a socially responsible business: how do you persuade your employees to buy into the company's social mission when so many of them simply came in search of a paycheck and a little security?

Sharing your passion and your knowledge with your employees

What employees want (and need) the most is to be treated with dignity and respect as intelligent human beings capable of making their own contributions to the success of the company. They crave appreciation and recognition. They value these experiences highly in all surveys of employee attitudes about their jobs. According to an extensive survey of employee attitudes conducted by Randstad, one of the world's largest job placement firms, more than nine out of ten workers value being trusted to do their jobs far more highly than how much they're paid. The most meaningful ways you can demonstrate that trust to your employees are to express your own personal appreciation for work well done, to train your managers to use positive instead of negative reinforcement to improve employee performance, and to include your workers in the company's decision-making processes as much as feasible. An involving, consultative style of management—within limits—will help you get the most from your investment in your employees.

If your company has a board of directors or advisers, you might also consider arranging for the nonmanagerial employees to elect one or more representatives to participate in board meetings. Under some circumstances, this may limit the information you can freely share with your board and introduce some awkwardness into discussions. On the whole, however, you're likely to find that this practice improves communication between the company's leadership and its rank-and-file employees and conveys a sense of trust to them. It helps minimize the adversarial relationship that tends to develop. That has been the case at Mal Warwick & Associates, where an employee representative is elected each year to serve on the board.

"Open-book management" is another of a number of methods that allow an owner or manager to involve employees meaningfully in making decisions for the business. In its purest form, this technique requires that every employee has access to all the company's financial reports as issued (whether monthly or quarterly). To assist workers in understanding the financials, an open-book manager will train them in interpreting the reports so that every employee understands every line of the profit-and-loss statement and the balance sheet. Often, employees are also offered courses in accounting, as well. But that's only part of the process, and in many ways a minor one. Open-book management also requires an elaborate system of target setting, department by department, on a monthly or quarterly basis—an exercise that draws a direct and unmistakably clear line between the performance of individual employees and the company's financial bottom line. The system works best when the company is either employee owned or has a strong and equitable profit-sharing plan that brings immediate rewards to all. When fully implemented under these circumstances, open-book management can truly turn even entry-level employees into business partners.

Consultative management, board representation, and open-book management are three of a number of approaches that are widely used to convey a sense to employees that their day-to-day efforts make a difference for the company as a whole. When sincerely employed, they can work well. In a values-driven business, however, helping workers understand that they have a stake in the company's fortunes isn't enough. By definition your business is based on *values*. Your job as owner or manager—and your greatest challenge—is to help your employees gain as deep and passionate a commitment to those values as you have.

There is no cut-and-dried method to accomplish this. It's not even enough to identify the company's values in an open meeting with employees because inevitably some of them will take little interest in this exercise—and you're likely to hire new employees who didn't share in this experience. Nor is personal charisma necessarily the key to successful motivation. (In many circumstances, charisma is a drawback. People can easily write off a charismatic leader as someone who's "different.") Employee motivation at this most basic level is built on an understanding of the difference between leadership and management:

- A manager may seek to regulate employees' behavior. A leader seeks to inspire them.

- All too often, a manager imposes unnecessary structure and hems employees in with rules that constrain their initiative. A leader welcomes and encourages initiative.

- A manager is prone to be preoccupied with day-to-day concerns such as quarterly earnings or the annual budget. A leader looks to the company's long-term prospects.

- A manager's approach to values may be to *explain* them. A leader tells stories about the company that *show* those values in action.

- A leader demonstrates a single-minded focus on the company's values, using failures as well as successes to illustrate the importance of making decisions that are consistent with the company's core values.

In most companies, management and leadership must merge in one or a handful of individuals. In your business, that means you. If you want your company to reflect your values consistently, you'll have to find a way to integrate insights such as these into your day-to-day behavior. And if you do, you'll discover that similar approaches will work with your contractors and suppliers, as well. That's the topic of the following chapter.

Turning Your Employees into Partners: A Checklist

Use this checklist as a quick guide to the steps you might take to boost employee morale, raise productivity, and improve customer service—by giving your employees a bigger stake in your business, both emotional and financial.

Policy or practice	Adopt?
Put a profit-sharing plan in place, distributing a meaningful share (at least 10 percent) of quarterly or annual profits to all qualified employees (e.g., those who have been on the payroll for a specified period of time, those who work full-time).	☐
Institute a program to provide employees with equity in the business, through either an employee stock ownership plan or some other means.	☐

Policy or practice	Adopt?
Provide for the election of a nonmanagement employee to your board of directors.	☐
Read Jack Stack's book *The Great Game of Business* to familiarize yourself with open-book management and determine whether it makes sense for your company.	☐
Visit ACORN's Living Wage Web site (http://www. livingwagecampaign.org) to learn about living-wage standards and how to determine the living wage for your business.	☐
Working with selected managers and employees, prepare a "wish list" of employment benefits that your company doesn't already offer. Then poll your employees to learn the priorities they place on those potential benefits. As conditions allow, implement these benefits starting at the top of the list.	☐
With your managers or selected employees, brainstorm ways that the company might offer new employment benefits at little or no cost.	☐
With outside assistance if necessary, explore the extent to which your company is successful in promoting diversity and inclusion among the employees and discuss ways you might improve your performance in this area.	☐
Institute a system by which employees may make suggestions for improvements in any area of the company's operations without fear of reprisal—in writing, if necessary, but ideally in an open forum or through an employee representative to your board.	☐
At least once annually, hold an all-staff meeting to discuss ways in which the company might improve its social-bottom-line performance.	☐

4

Turning the value chain into a "values chain"

The advocates of the dog-eat-dog school of capitalism contend that just three criteria should be considered when selecting contractors or suppliers: price, quality, and reliability. But if you think that's the way American consumers think, just ask Nike or the Gap what happened to their sales when some of the factories producing goods for them were exposed for unfair labor practices. Both those companies, having learned the hard way that the American public cares how employees are treated, have since set out to become model corporate citizens.

"Now, hold on!" you might be saying. Sweatshops, child labor, and sixteen-hour-a-day jobs at ten cents an hour represent the extreme case. "Good old Frank's Machine Shop, which has been supplying our widgets for years, isn't some Third World sweatshop!"

Fair enough. In most instances, the contractors and suppliers you deal with day after day are reasonable people who run their businesses in full compliance with the law and treat their employees well. They may belong to the Better Business Bureau, the local chamber of commerce, or the Rotary Club and go to the same church, synagogue, or mosque as you. They're good people, right?

Here's the rub: if you're running a values-driven business—if you're committed to making the world a better place—then you'll want to consider all the ways you can live your values through your business. If you treat your employees the way they want to be treated, emphasize diversity and inclusion in hiring and in your management style, offer only goods and services that provide your customers with true value, involve yourself and your coworkers in supporting your community, and take pains to minimize your company's impact on the environment, you'll discover that your investment in these efforts will pay off richly and in unexpected ways. It's hard to find a more powerful message to take to good old Frank down at the machine shop! By the force of your example and the strength of your enthusiasm, you may be able to persuade your contractors and suppliers that they, too, would benefit from a values-driven approach.

Imprinting your values on your suppliers

Consider old Frank, for example. An on-site inspection, a few open-ended questions, and a little patience might turn up any one or more of the following circumstances:

- Frank's little shop has had constant employee turnover for twenty-five years. For some reason—low pay? poor working conditions? bad management?—Frank's younger machinists have been leaving after short periods of time to set up their own shops. Most of Frank's competition now consists of these unplanned spin-offs. You've stuck with Frank out of sheer loyalty. But maybe those widgets you've been buying from him for years could be had at competitive, or even lower prices from one of those competitors with less staff turnover and a more contemporary approach to management. Or maybe Frank just assumes that losing employees is a natural part of his business and is unaware that his own management practices are at fault.

- Much to your surprise, you discover that Frank's shop is filthy. That in itself may mean nothing, but it could be a signal that Frank is careless, or even downright uncaring, about disposing of the used lubricants and solvents that are so widely used in his business. In fact, if Frank has been around for long enough and has been heedless of good practices in the disposal of toxic chemicals, he might be responsible for his own little potential Superfund site. (You think this is far-fetched? Check out what's happened in your community after a dry cleaner or a gasoline station has closed down and someone has tried to make use of the same site for a different sort of business.) If you feel strongly about minimizing your company's impact on the environment, then you may want to rethink doing business with Frank.

- Your commitment to equal opportunity, a consequence of the importance you place on your core value of fairness, is challenged when you learn that all Frank's employees are Caucasian in a part of your community that's remarkably diverse ethnically and racially. What, then, is the net effect of your company's pledge to be a showcase for equal opportunity? That commitment goes only as far as the boundaries of your work site. You may want to look around more widely for a machine shop that's competitive with Frank's but is run in a way that's more consistent with your values. Or Frank may be willing to institute a program to promote diversity and inclusion in his shop. After all, he may simply be unaware that there are simple, straightforward, and inexpensive steps he could take to increase diversity in his company—and you may be able to help him identify them.

By taking a close look at your contractors and suppliers, you may discover that they violate your values. Such discoveries offer you a range of choices. You can seek to work with a vendor in hopes of helping the management improve its performance and more closely conform to the values you respect. You can switch vendors if you recognize that the chances are slim that you could persuade the present ownership or management to make the necessary changes. Or you can take a much broader view entirely of your supply chain and seek to help make the world a better place by choosing suppliers that reflect your values in exemplary ways.

Sometimes, in fact, collaboration with one or another of your suppliers can produce mutual benefits of great value. For instance, Ben & Jerry's contracted with Greyston Bakery (see chapter 6) to produce the brownies for its Chocolate Fudge Brownie ice cream. From Ben's perspective, this was one of the best decisions the company ever made. It was meaningful to marry a social benefit to the community—through Greyston— to the day-to-day process of making ice cream. Simply adding another criterion (social benefit) to its sourcing specifications of price and quality enabled Ben & Jerry's to help build a company whose purpose was to hire formerly unemployable people. For more than a decade now, Ben & Jerry's has continued to be one of Greyston's biggest accounts.

Or consider another example—the case of Avalon Natural Products.

Avalon Natural Products
Win-Win Solutions through Collaboration

Avalon Natural Products is the leading brand of natural and organic body and skin care products in the natural products industry. It sports three brands: Avalon Organics, Alba, and Unpetroleum.

In 2004, the company learned that scientists from the European Economic Union identified and banned more than 1,135 toxic chemicals being used in personal and home care products, categorizing them as carcinogens, reproductive toxins, and mutagens. Although the U.S. Food and Drug Administration had banned only nine such chemicals (versus a total ban by the European Community) in 2004, Avalon last year decided to take the lead and reformulate close to 100 items in the Avalon Organics line to eliminate all toxic ingredients. That meant working in close partnership with the company's vendors, the manufacturers of Avalon's products.

"We developed a mission called Consciousness in Cosmetics, and our mantra is 'Honor your body with consciousness,'" says Morris Shriftman, senior vice president of marketing and new product development, who has been in charge of the reformulation project. "We want people to understand that the skin is the largest organ and much of what you put on it is absorbed directly into your body. Women can use as many as fifteen to twenty-five personal care products every day. Even small amounts of toxic substances can accumulate in the body and create problems."

Avalon's consciousness-raising mission has applied to both consumers and vendors alike. Working in tandem with the Breast Cancer Fund, the company collaborated with its suppliers to completely remove unhealthy chemicals, such as parabens, petroleum-based substances, urea, and artificial colors and fragrances, from products produced for Avalon and to create safer, cleaner, purer personal care products with enhanced levels of organic ingredients, such as essential oils and certified organic vegetable oils. "We asked our suppliers to completely rethink their use of ingredients and how they put them together—something that was totally new and very difficult—but we received tremendous support from them," says Shriftman. "They were excited about the process because they were collaborating with us to do something that was truly outstanding and that would positively affect the lives of millions of customers."

It's been a win-win deal for everyone involved. "The product reformulation has ended up helping our suppliers in their own businesses," says Shriftman. "Now they have unique formulation abilities that they can bring to other clients, as well." Avalon continues to work with vendors to support the increase of the acreage under organic cultivation, reduce unnecessary packaging, and make sure that products are not environmentally polluting.

Avalon readily gained its suppliers' cooperation. But that may not always be the case. Sometimes you have to switch suppliers to conduct your business in a way that's fully consistent with your values.

Choosing vendors who will make a difference

If you're a retailer committed to a just and sustainable future, obtaining products from distributors or processors who favor "fair trade" suppliers for their raw materials is an ideal option.

If you've pledged to make your products or services available to everyone in your community, then one consideration you may wish to take into account when choosing vendors is whether they have a diverse workforce (in terms of race, ethnicity, sexual orientation, gender, age, and physical ability).

If you wish to narrow the economic inequities in your community, then selecting contractors, vendors, or suppliers that are minority or woman owned is a small but important step for you—significant in its own right but, more importantly, emblematic of your core values.

If you want to know whether your suppliers are part of the problem of our environmental challenges—or part of the solution—ask them. Prepare a simple questionnaire to determine the extent to which they have implemented environmentally friendly practices in their own businesses—and make it clear that your decisions about sourcing in the future will be based in part on what you learn.

These are just a few of the ways that you can bring your values to the fore when you consider vendors for your business—whether they're entirely new vendors or alternatives to your current suppliers. Not that such a course is likely to be easy: for example, many companies have learned that doing business with minority- or woman-owned firms (which are often smaller and newer than most of their competitors) has required significant effort to help them meet quality and on-time delivery standards. In some cases, values-driven businesses have loaned money or made equity investments in such suppliers to help them obtain the facilities or hire the new staff needed to meet quality standards.

Just as consumers are quickly learning that the money they spend for goods and services represents leverage for change in business, many small and midsized businesses are coming to understand what major corporations have long known: that their dollars, too, represent a potential force for change. But don't get the impression that you'll always have to pressure or threaten your suppliers to uphold your values. Sometimes, as Pura Vida Coffee has found, they may be eager to work with you *because* of your values.

Pura Vida Coffee
Shared Values

Pura Vida Coffee, founded in 1998 and headquartered in Seattle, is the premier sustainable beverage company that appeals to values-driven consumers. It offers a full array of coffee, tea, cocoa, chai, and other products that have been sustainably grown and produced by growers who are paid premium prices. Profits from the company, which is held and wholly owned by Pura Vida Partners, a public charity, are distributed in the countries and communities where the products are sourced and also fund Pura Vida's own philanthropic programs.

"Vendors have chosen to work with us in large part because of our model," says John Sage, president and cofounder. "We've created an entity that has the discipline, rigor, and accountability of a for-profit yet whose intent is charitable. The coffee company is the money-generating engine that funds the philanthropic activity of the parent organization. It's also something of a 'Trojan horse' for introducing customers to our mission and charitable work and to the importance of buying fair-trade goods that allow the producers to be paid a living wage."

Pura Vida works to provide physical and emotional nourishment for at-risk children in coffee-growing countries. In Costa Rica, six full-time staff run programs in four communities, helping 400 to 500 children a day receive food, computer education, and other arts and sports enrichment to help keep them off the streets. Young mothers also are provided with free mental-health counseling. This fall, Pura Vida will grant fifty educational scholarships to children of coffee farmers in Ethiopia, as well.

"We're tough-minded and tenderhearted, trying to be simultaneously about the bottom line and social impact," Sage says.

Pura Vida buys only fair-trade coffee, paying a minimum price that is substantially above the commodity prices for coffee in a dozen countries. This helps guarantee a living wage for coffee farmers, who have suffered from historically low commodity prices over the past several years as well as further economic hardship due to the vagaries of the market. One of Pura Vida's most important vendors is Cooperative Coffees, a nonprofit comprising fourteen roaster-retailers, which sources the green coffee around the world. Membership in the cooperative allows Pura Vida and other participating companies to benefit from the combined volume of their purchases to gain efficiencies in shipping and storage. "There is very much a shared set of values between Cooperative Coffees and Pura Vida, a strong commitment to creating a sustainable economic model for coffee producers," Sage says. "The founder, Bill Harris, has a devoted heart for the developing world."

Because of Pura Vida and fair trade, a producer who was once able to earn only $10 for 100 pounds of coffee and who was forced to take her children out of school to help in the fields is now able to receive over $85 for the same amount and keep her children in school. More demand for fair-trade coffee will ensure that more farmers are able to sell their entire crop at fair trade prices.

"Vendors are attracted to the idea that we're using the discipline and the tools of business to compete in the marketplace in order to change lives like that," Sage says.

Pura Vida's other vendors include the roasters who turn the beans from green to brown. One of them, Dillanos, agreed initially to sell coffee to Pura Vida at a discount to help support the company in its work. "Our volumes have grown thirty times since then, and so it's turned out to be a good deal for them," says Sage.

Another vendor, of sorts, is Sysco, the large food distributor, which brings Pura Vida Coffee into colleges, churches, and businesses. "They made it clear when they sought us out a year ago that it was the intensity of our commitment to sustainability that attracted them to us," Sage notes.

"I definitely view our vendors as partners," he says. "They're almost like family. We spend countless days, weeks, and hours with them, and we all know each other very well. We're lucky that they share our passion and goals."

Pura Vida's experience with its suppliers is not unusual. Many other companies, acting on the belief that people in business will jump at the chance to make a difference, have discovered their vendors to be willing partners in adding social value to their work. A young cosmetics company called PeaceKeeper has had a similar experience.

PeaceKeeper Cause-Metics
Putting Your Money Where Your Mouth Is

"Look Good, Feel Good, Do Good." That's the motto of Peace-Keeper Cause-Metics, the first cosmetics company in history to give all its after-tax profits to support women's health advocacy and human rights issues. By purchasing PeaceKeeper products, women can help make a difference on issues such as rape, female genital mutilation, honor killings, and female infanticide, as well as on illnesses affecting women such as heart disease, autoimmune disease, and cancer.

Based in New York City and launched in April 2002, the company features nail polishes and lip products, including PeaceKeeper V-Day Gloss, whose proceeds support the activities of *Vagina Monologues* playwright Eve Ensler's V-Day campaign to end violence against women, and PeaceKeeper Unifem Gloss, whose proceeds go to the United Nations Trust Fund to Eliminate Violence Against Women.

PeaceKeeper will soon be devoting a quarter of its funds to supporting public education on the issue of the sex-slave trade for a two-year period and will solicit customers for advice on where to give away the remaining funds. Meanwhile, as the company is ramping up to profitability, it is giving one-half of

1 percent of its gross revenues each year to support advocacy against domestic violence. And PeaceKeeper has donated approximately $30,000 in products to nonprofit silent auctions.

PeaceKeeper has benefited from extraordinary relationships with vendors, buyers, and public relations firms. "Michael Warford of Colts Plastic and treasurer of Cosmetic Industry Buyers and Suppliers, CIBS, has been extraordinarily helpful in introducing us to vendors who don't gouge our margins and who resonate with our mission," says founder and CEO Jody Weiss. Those vendors, she notes, have also worked closely with PeaceKeeper to develop packaging that uses recycled paper and to create unique product formulations based on minerals that come from the earth. "Our products don't have harmful chemicals, FD&C coloring, or preservatives and are not tested on animals," Weiss says.

Nordstrom has been a helpful collaborator with Peace-Keeper, as well, providing visibility and positioning for the young product line, including in-store promotions featuring celebrities such as actress Bree Williamson. "The buyers and saleswomen at Nordstrom see themselves as cocreators with us in building a company that will eventually give away millions of dollars to support women around the world," Weiss says.

Finally, a top-of-the-line New York–based boutique public relations firm, Red PR, has agreed to work with Weiss—frequently on a pro bono basis. The firm's assiduous efforts to see that PeaceKeeper's line attracts support at swanky venues such as the Golden Globe Awards, the American Music Awards, and the Daytime Emmy Awards have led to numerous celebrity endorsements. "The firm believes in what we're doing and knows that the payback will come when our company takes off, which it is very much poised to do," says Weiss.

"Our collaborators are helping us make it possible for women who want for nothing to use their discretionary buying power to improve the lives of women who can't even *afford* a lipstick," says Weiss. That's what you might call putting your money where your mouth is.

Where does social change start?

Maybe right about now you're thinking, "Look, guys, all this stuff about values and socially responsible business and 'suppliers' is a little over my head. I'm running a small office with seven employees, and we don't even *have* suppliers. We're not General Motors, you know?"

Well, guess again. Most businesses, no matter how small, depend on *someone else* for something. Here are just a few of the possibilities to take into account:

- The bank that holds the mortgage on your space or has loaned you working capital

- The janitorial service that cleans your office once or twice a week

- The messenger service that makes urgent local deliveries for you

- The shipping company that moves your packages longer distances

- The stationery store or office supplier that sells you paper and paper clips

- The company that provides your telephone service

- The computer store or online source where you buy computer equipment, software, and accessories

- The accountant or tax preparation service you use

- The attorney who consults with you when tough decisions come up

When you stop to think about it, you're really not in business alone. Your little business is at the center of a web of relationships with many other companies. You have the opportunity to explore the potential for leverage in every one of these relationships to help make the world a better place. For example:

- Some banks are immeasurably better than others in lending to the communities where they're located, promoting diversity among their employees, supporting only environmentally desirable development projects, and a host of other areas. Check out your bank's business policies and practices. If you have a choice, consider switching if necessary. Check out ShoreBank if you're in the Chicago or Detroit or Portland, Oregon, areas. Good behavior needs to be rewarded!

- One of the few businesses that recent immigrants and people of color find it easy to enter is the janitorial services business. If the company that serves your business is a large, commercial service, take a look around town. You might well find a bonded, minority-owned business that will do the job at least as well—and possibly even for less money.

- Some messenger services use gas-guzzling trucks. Perhaps a bicycle messenger service is available locally, or at least a company that does a little less damage to the atmosphere.

- The shipping business is highly competitive. As in every industry, some companies are better than others when it comes to labor relations, environmental policies, and other matters of potential concern. If you're dealing with a nationwide company, check it out online. You may learn something that will move you to switch—or to stick it out where you are.

- Office supplies, especially paper, are commodities—but you'll find significant differences. One hundred percent postconsumer recycled paper, which is typically a little more expensive than paper made from virgin pulp, is available from some suppliers but not all. Look around. You may find an office supply source that will meet your needs for quality, on-time delivery, and responsiveness—and make you feel a little better about your impact on the environment, too. The perfect supplier for you if you're located in northern California may be Give Something Back Business Products.

- Since the telephone industry was deregulated many years ago, competition has become more and more a reality. Some telephone service providers offer essential services at competitive rates (or better) while contributing their profits to nonprofit organizations working for positive social change. For instance, you might check out two remarkable SVN-affiliated companies, BetterWorld Telecom and Working Assets Long Distance.

- Some computer manufacturers are immeasurably better than others in terms of their stakeholder policies. They often generate immense amounts of revenue, which can do a lot of good or a lot of something else. For example, Hewlett-Packard, one of the world's biggest computer makers, has long been an innovator in corporate social responsibility.

- It may be difficult for you to implement values-driven business policies and practices without active support from your accountant and your attorney. If they resist—and if one or both of them aren't your wife's sisters or cousins—it might be time to shop around.

These are just a few of the innumerable possibilities that will turn up if you use a little imagination. For hundreds of others, check out Co-op America's *National Green Pages*, which lists thousands of businesses all across the country that practice the values we're writing about here. Your own company may qualify for a listing, too!

Historians and social scientists have lots of fancy things to say about social change. They've got more theories than you can fit in the upstairs closet. Truth to tell, though, social change isn't usually about the grand political revolutions that get so much attention in the history books or even about technological changes, either. Those are both major factors in promoting the phenomenon, but they're not its essence. Social change occurs when people alter their daily habits, when they start to look at familiar things in unfamiliar ways. That's really what values-driven business is about.

One of the most effective ways that you and your company can become an agent of social change is to reexamine your relationships with your suppliers, vendors, and contractors. It's amazing how much influence you can wield with only a little purchasing power. But sometimes all it takes is to communicate clearly what you're trying to achieve through your business. You may find that the folks you know are more receptive to change than you ever imagined.

Now, please join us in chapter 5, as we begin to explore another dimension of values-based business: your customers.

Partnering with Your Suppliers: a Checklist

Use this checklist as a menu of the actions you might take to advance your company's mission and honor your values by choosing your vendors or contractors more carefully or collaborating with them more closely.

Policy or practice	Adopt?
Make a list of all the contractors, vendors, and suppliers that serve your business. Determine how many of them represent ownership by people of color or women.	☐
Prepare a short questionnaire about employment practices, covering any issues of interest to you, including matters such as employee ownership, diversity and inclusion policies, job benefits, profit sharing, and the like. Canvass your contractors and suppliers using this questionnaire.	☐
List the ways that suppliers or contractors might contribute to the community. Ask them how many of these activities or practices apply to them.	☐
Quiz your suppliers, vendors, and contractors about their environmental practices. Figure out how well they meet your own company's high standards in this field.	☐
Investigate whether a promising woman- or minority-owned firm might meet your company's needs as a supplier if it receives technical or financial assistance from you.	☐
Determine whether your contractors and suppliers are aware of the vision, mission, and values of your company. Share that information with them. If desirable, offer a tour of your facility to provide them with a fuller understanding of the values that drive your business.	☐
If your company works with suppliers outside the United States, make site visits to their facilities to satisfy yourself that their business practices are consistent with your values. If necessary, contract with an agency such as Verité to investigate on your behalf.	☐
Conduct a survey in your community to learn whether any businesses or nonprofits that hire the disabled might provide you with necessary goods or services.	☐

Policy or practice	Adopt?
Produce a flyer or brochure that clearly sets forth your company's vision, mission, and values, and distribute it to all your existing vendors and contractors. (Include it with your marketing materials, too!)	☐
Ask each of your vendors for a list of the ingredients it uses in its products. Are they nontoxic, natural, or organic? Do they use recycled materials? Do their products contain any known or suspected carcinogens?	☐

5

Developing a dialogue with your customers

In a business—any business—there is a relationship between the company and its customers. In a successful business, that relationship unfolds in a series of stages that bring customers back again and again. But in a values-driven business, the relationship between company and customer sometimes reaches an even deeper level, where the two become partners in meeting the needs of the community, the nation, or the environment. That, we believe, is the ideal to which a socially responsible business can aspire.

In the table labeled "Who's on First?" you'll see one schematic way to look at the development of the relationship between a company and its customers as time goes by.

Any business, no matter how small, whether socially responsible or not, seeks to develop strong, continuing relationships with its customers. Nothing is inherently "responsible" about that. It's just good business.

You can't get around it, though: if the values on which you're building your business don't include some special consideration for your customers, you have to ask yourself why you are in business:

Who's on First?

Stage	What happens	Why
1	Customer buys product or service	The company has done at least a minimally adequate job of providing something the customer needs or wants. Something's working: either the price is right, the quality is acceptable, the product or service is available at a convenient time and place, or some combination of these circumstances holds true.
2	Customer repeatedly returns to buy product or service	Brand loyalty is developing. The company has succeeded in communicating to the customer that one or more aspects of the product or service are more satisfying than what competitors can offer: either the nature of the product itself, its quality, its price, the convenience of its availability, or the service values associated with the product. The customer is responding to the company's brand "personality," not just the external attributes of its product or service.
3	Customer takes an active interest in the company, helping recruit new customers through word of mouth	The company has successfully conveyed its values to at least some of its customers. Its product or service has become not simply a preferred brand but an expression of the customer's values. Though largely unvoiced, a genuine dialogue occurs between company and customer.
4	Customer joins the company in actions to improve the quality of life in their shared community; to address a social need locally, nationally, or internationally; or to preserve the environment	If the company has achieved stage 3, then it's easy to move on to stage 4. The company has reached out to its customers, offering one or more ways that company and customer together can make a difference in the world. Both company and customer are acting on their values—shared values. The values dialogue between the two has matured into an active partnership.

- Are you running a company just to make a buck—or to deliver superior goods and services to people who need them and make a profit in the process?

- If customers really come first, how far are you prepared to go to meet their needs?

- If you want your company to be known for quality and service, what are the limits, if any, that you'll place on satisfying unhappy customers?

The experience at Seventh Generation casts light on some of these questions, showing one company's innovative approach to its customers.

Seventh Generation
Building Trust

Seventh Generation, founded in 1988, is the leading brand of nontoxic and environmentally safe household and personal care products. The company has become a leader in the corporate effort to preserve the environment, garnering fifteen major awards recognizing its work in this arena.

"Our mission is not necessarily to sell to people who are completely aligned with our values," says Jeffrey Hollender, president and corporate responsibility officer. "Our goal is to have a dialogue with people that perhaps helps them to see the world in a different way or empowers them to have the impact they want to have on the world."

Seventh Generation boasts six core values: creating trust in the Seventh Generation brand, offering "Wow!" service, promoting social and environmental responsibility, providing opportunities for personal growth and fulfillment on the part of staff, improving the community, and modeling corporate leadership—that is, being a force for positive social change in the markets the company serves. Seventh Generation spends a good deal of time articulating its values and determining whether the organization is operating in harmony with them.

"Wow!" service has to do with understanding—and trying to exceed—customers' needs and expectations. Those customers include both retailers (large retail chains such as Whole Foods, Target, and Kroger) and the ultimate consumers.

"You build trust by doing things like listening, fulfilling your commitments, and being honest," Hollender says. One of the factors that distinguish Seventh Generation as a company is authenticity. When the preservative in one of their dish-washing liquid products failed, for example, leaving customers with a goop smelling like rotten eggs, Seventh Generation immediately pulled the product off the shelves and addressed the issue in detail in its consumer newsletter. "We didn't hide that we screwed up," Hollender says. "That's value in the world we live in." In fact, that's value in just about anybody's world.

Seventh Generation's view on customer feedback? "The more the better," says Hollender. "We understand that the brand lives with the customer, not with us. What they think is what matters, not what we say about ourselves." That's why all Seventh Generation products include the company's phone number and e-mail address on the packaging. The organization also sends special e-mails to customers notifying them when Hollender is speaking in the neighborhood.

"Transparency is the foundation of good relationships with customers," he says. "We're constantly looking for new ways to share information about ourselves with our stake-holders. We work with customers, nonprofits, vendors, and retailers in asking, 'What is it that you want to know about us?' We publish our turnover rate, for example, so that people can know every year how many employees left the company as a percentage of our total workforce, because we think that's a real indicator of the kind of experience and fulfillment that our staff are having.

"When we commit ourselves to sharing information with the public, we become increasingly focused, and that's a good thing for us," Hollender says.

For Seventh Generation, listening to customers is an indispensable marketing tool. For you and your company, learning from the market can be the key to success. But the lengths to which Seventh Generation goes to satisfy unhappy customers raises a very practical question you'll face sooner or later, or perhaps every day: should you put a limit on how far you'll go to keep customers happy?

You want *what*? You want it *when*?

It's not just good business to do your utmost to satisfy your customers. In a values-driven business, it also reflects a commitment to provide genuine value to clients or customers, not simply sell as much as possible and as easily as possible. But customers represent just one of the five dimensions of values-driven business. What happens when your commitment to your customers collides with an equal or even stronger commitment to another stakeholder group?

Consider this scenario.

You're doing your level best to run your business in a way that's fully consistent with the lofty values that bring meaning to your life and the lives of your employees. You've got in place all sorts of great policies and practices. You're getting a lot of good feedback from all sides. But somehow, not quite everybody is getting the message that you and your employees are really *special*. They seem to think that you're just like any other business. Imagine that!

For example, a customer walks in with that familiar swagger and a sneer on his face, ignoring the large sign that looms above the counter advising customers that one-day service requires payment of a rush fee. Once again, he demands in a loud voice that his job be returned before the end of the afternoon and refuses to pay any rush fee. The sales rep who's working at the counter knows he's one of your biggest customers. She wants to be accommodating, even though she finds him consistently abusive. In fact, business is a little slow today.

What would you have that sales rep do? How would you handle the situation if you were called to the counter to deal with that abusive customer?

At Mal Warwick & Associates, a consulting firm with an average of two dozen clients at any given time, the policy that evolved over the years was to limit doing business with genuinely troublesome clients. Clients that demonstrate a pattern of abuse to the company's staff are "fired," no matter the financial consequences. (When you terminate a contract with 5 percent of your customers, you might feel the impact!) Those that make consistently unreasonable demands on staff time—for example, by insisting on endless rounds of changes in copy or artwork—are asked to stop doing so or pay substantially higher fees. In its business development, one of the company's criteria for taking on new clients is the staff's judgment about how smoothly they might work with the people who work for the client.

At Ben & Jerry's, employees dealing with customers were asked to be increasingly nicer and more accommodating with angry customers, hoping to win them over with kindness. That usually worked, but if a customer made a habit of nasty behavior, a manager intervened to ask the customer to leave.

Naturally, if every customer were like that abusive guy with the swagger, business would be no fun at all. Most of us wouldn't dream of exposing ourselves to treatment like that on a daily basis. In fact, when we do at least a reasonably good job of serving our customers, business is pleasant, rewarding—and often fun. But, as any book on the fundamentals of business will tell you, it's not enough to satisfy the minimal requirements of your customers. For your company to excel, you've got to listen to them, too. If your company is truly committed to adding value to your customers, you've got no choice in the matter.

Sometimes, in fact, a company's values come through clearly just in the attentive way it caters to a niche market, demonstrating a community of interest that encompasses more than merely the needs that are filled by its products. Consider, for instance, the case of Warm Spirit.

Warm Spirit
Listening to Customers

Warm Spirit has been all about customers since day one. When Nadine Thompson and Daniel Wolf were tossing around the idea of creating a company, they decided that addressing the needs of an underserved group—African-American women— was the way to go. "In the Black community, we usually get only the cheapest, lousiest stuff for hair and body care," says Thompson, Warm Spirit president and CEO. "I thought, why not create high-quality, nature-based products that specifically address the needs of people who look like me?"

Starting with six recipes for lotions and soap in 1999, the company now produces and sells more than 350 products devoted to body care, wellness, and health care. Some 14,000 consultants market and distribute the products through direct sales all over the country. Most of those consultants are themselves African-American women and for Warm Spirit compose a customer base just as important as the company's end users. "We're doing for African-American women entrepreneurs and clients what Mary Kay did for white women," Thompson says. The company supports its consultants through free semiweekly coaching sessions held over the telephone as well as larger regional trainings.

Warm Spirit has built a solid reputation with consumers by attending to the special personal care requirements of African Americans. "Black skin and hair tend to dry out more easily, so we put more nourishing oils in our products," says Thompson. "People can use our lotions, soaps, shampoos, and conditioners knowing that they'll end up glowing." Customers are drawn not only to Warm Spirit's essential oils and all-natural ingredients but also to the idea that through their own buying power they can help support women-owned businesses in their own community. "They recognize that they're helping to build the local economy," says Thompson.

Thompson herself, backed up by a customer service team, encourages clients to e-mail her personally with their feedback. "Most of it has to do with how incredibly grateful people are that they now have quality natural products available to them," she says. Complaints are handled with prompt e-mail responses and appropriate interventions. "One of the best things you can do for your customers is give a money-back guarantee," she notes. Bigger issues—such as the famous Warm Spirit "body polish" that tends to leak during shipping—are handled either by making changes in production processes or by advising consultants to give customers fair warning. "We tell the truth," says Thompson.

Being attentive to specific customer needs and feedback has indeed resulted in success. The company currently does an impressive $1 million a month in sales. And it's not only African Americans who enjoy the products. People from a wide variety of backgrounds, including men, find the Warm Spirit line to be top-notch. "I'm married to a minister who once preached a sermon on the idea that when you pay attention to the small, it benefits all," Thompson says. "By being mindful of creating products that work for African Americans, we've in fact created products that work for everyone."

You could argue that Warm Spirit's success merely reflects good niche marketing and isn't necessarily socially responsible. You might need to know a lot more about how Nadine Thompson does business to understand that her company is deeply committed to a vision of a better world and is seeking to make it a reality through the way she operates Warm Spirit. But the company's truly attentive stance toward its customers is fundamental to the values system it brings to the marketplace. Other niche marketers might learn how to connect with their customers and deliver products or services that catch on. In most cases, however, the process ends there. At Warm Spirit and other values-driven businesses, that connection with customers makes it possible for the company to engage them in a deeper dialogue. But the process starts with listening.

Are your eyes and ears always open?

We confess. Listening to customers doesn't *necessarily* reflect socially responsible values. It *does* to the extent that the satisfaction and well-being of customers rank high in your values hierarchy. But without an intimate understanding of customers' wants, needs, and values, it's difficult, perhaps impossible, to gain the level of trust that's required before your customers will be willing to listen to what you have to say. You've got to get past the basics before you can get fancy.

But how can you gain that understanding? What does "listening" really mean in practice?

A major corporation is likely to have a marketing department with its own in-house research capabilities—or a big enough marketing budget to hire a top-flight agency to provide those services. That's even the case at many midsized companies. But lacking those resources is no excuse to ignore the invaluable insight you can gain from systematically encouraging and evaluating customer feedback. Here are just a few of the many techniques you might adopt at little or no cost:

- As the company's owner or manager, make occasional phone calls to your biggest customers—or, if you don't have key customers, to a random sample of those who buy your products or services. Quiz them on whether they're satisfied with your work—and ask how well your employees are treating them.

- Once each year, pay a visit to your key customers to discuss with them face-to-face how satisfied they are with your company.

- Set up a toll-free number for customer complaints or suggestions. Nowadays a toll-free number costs very little.

- In the event that any problem arises with one of your products or services, be transparent. Take immediate action to recall products and correct problems if safety or health risks occur or if quality is poor.

- Invite your customers to send their questions, comments, or complaints via your company's Web site. Respond to all communications promptly—first, with a bounce-back e-mail message to thank the customer for writing, then with a message that specifically addresses the customer's concern.

- Appoint an ombudsperson to follow up on customer inquiries and complaints and ensure that customers are taken good care of.

- Produce a short quiz on customer satisfaction and include it in your packages or (in the case of services) your invoices.

- Once a year, survey your customers to elicit their attitudes and ideas about your service. If you have few customers, include them all in the survey. If you have many customers, select a random sample. Always follow up on signed complaints.

- Set up a log to record the essentials about each incoming call from customers, including the date, time, identity of the caller, nature of the comment or question, and product or service involved. Review the log carefully once a month, and monitor it on an ongoing basis to track trends and look for shifts in customer attitudes.

Activities like these will get you started. But it's just a start because listening to your customers reflects only one side of the picture. In a strong customer relationship, a dialogue of sorts occurs on several levels. Your guarantee (or whatever assurances you make to customers about your products or services) communicates a set of qualities about your work that can help inspire the sort of trust that Jeffrey Hollender speaks about—so long as your claims match the reality. The character of your communications with customers creates another level of trust. If you are open and honest about matters such as defects or errors, service deficiencies, delivery delays, and cost overruns or price increases, your customers are likely to be more forgiving when trouble arises. But yet another level of communication exists, one that may play an even larger role in fostering the trust that is the heart of our relationships with the lifelong customers we all want to acquire.

Leading with your values

That deeper level of communication is a dialogue—often a silent dialogue—on the level of values. Any company that has developed trust with its customers can actively engage in this dialogue and make use of it as a vehicle to promote its values.

Consumer-products companies like Ben & Jerry's and Stonyfield Farm can use their packaging to deliver messages that embody their values and support the causes they care about. They also have big enough marketing budgets to advertise over the airwaves or in print media.

For instance, Ben & Jerry's came up with a product called Peace Pops. Its packaging promoted the idea of using 1 percent of the Pentagon's budget to finance activities that supported peace through understanding. That didn't cost anything extra, but it set Ben & Jerry's apart from its competition and created the image of a caring, involved, activist company. It also generated a lot of PR value. But the company didn't launch Peace Pops to gain publicity or differentiate itself from its competitors. The product and its promotion were a natural outgrowth of the business's values. Peace Pops were introduced in a time before the end of the cold war, when Russia (then the Soviet Union) was thought to be a threat to U.S. security. After the Peace Pop came out, the cold war ended. (You'll have to judge for yourself whether there was a cause-and-effect relationship between the two.) Later, before the first Gulf War, the company bought space along with thirty other companies in the *New York Times* for an open letter to the president and Congress not to go to war. With promotions like these, there was no doubt in anyone's mind where Ben & Jerry's stood on issues of war and peace.

Some time later, Ben & Jerry's partnered with the Children's Defense Fund—the people who actually invented the phrase

"Leave No Child Behind"—before it was appropriated by a government that had always fought its proposals. Using means such as active distribution of promotional materials at its popular annual rock festivals, displays in its scoop shops, and promotions on its packaging, Ben & Jerry's helped the Children's Defense Fund recruit thousands of new members to support legislation protecting children's rights and providing them with essential services.

By wearing its values on its sleeve, Ben & Jerry's was able to build a consumer franchise that became the number one or number two bestselling super-premium ice cream in the country. The conventional wisdom in business is that if you're public about controversial issues—for example, taking a stand as Ben & Jerry's did on devoting a larger share of the federal budget to activities that would promote peace through understanding and less money to the Pentagon—then the business would suffer. It was presumed that people who don't agree with you won't buy your products. But Ben & Jerry's proved that advertising its values didn't hurt its business—in fact, quite the opposite, it drove the business.

Why might it work that way? Perhaps one-third of the people are motivated by a controversial stand a company takes—and that makes them better customers. Another third don't agree with the company, but that doesn't prevent them from buying ice cream (or whatever you're selling). And about a third don't care. That's not to say that Ben & Jerry's didn't receive hundreds of letters over the years from people claiming they wouldn't buy its ice cream because of some stand the company had taken. But those letters were overwhelmingly outnumbered by the thousands of others reporting that "we believe in what you're doing." And we have to admit to a little skepticism that all those naysayers really had the willpower to give up Cherry Garcia or Chunky Monkey.

Ben & Jerry's is by no means alone among socially responsible companies that have sought to lead with their values, advancing ideas or proposals for social or environmental change to their customers and inviting them to participate. For example:

■ Judy Wicks's White Dog Cafe (see chapter 6) is a brilliant example of a business that seizes every conceivable opportunity to use its position of trust with its customers to advance an issues agenda. The restaurant's list of issues spans humane treatment of animals, the value of locally grown and organic produce, the living-wage campaign, local living economies, opposition to U.S. military action when it seems unjustified, and indigenous rights in Mexico's state of Chiapas. To some, the list seems endless. For Wicks, there are few boundaries. She seeks to set a "table for six billion."

■ Working Assets Funding Service, which operates Working Assets Long Distance, doesn't just donate a large portion of its profits to support causes and institutions that reflect its values ($47 million to date)—it also uses its monthly telephone bills to customers to urge them to participate in one or more activist campaigns each month. And all that money the company gives away? Customers vote once a year on which nonprofit organizations will receive the funds.

■ Similarly, Give Something Back (see chapter 2) annually invites its customers to help identify which local charities will receive the funds it distributes to the communities where it does business.

■ Public relations company Fenton Communications doesn't just seek out clients that reflect the progressive political values of its founder and staff. It actively works with its clients to advance their work, highlighting many of their programs in its house organ, *Communiqué,* and on its Web site.

- Mal Warwick & Associates operates in a similar way, publicizing its clients' campaigns through its electronic newsletter and Web site, highlighting their work in its annual *Stakeholder's Report,* contributing funds to client campaigns, inviting clients' representatives to speak about their work at staff meetings, and inviting employees and friends to participate directly as activists, not just by providing professional services. The company also opens up its office from time to time to permit selected local political campaigns to stage phone banks to educate voters or urge them to go to the polls. And it participates in collective efforts with other businesses in taking public positions through advertising, communications with elected officials, and occasional lobbying before legislative bodies on issues that reflect the company's values.

As a small business, your company possesses a number of advantages over the corporations that dominate the commercial landscape. You have the ability to act more quickly on changes in technology and consumer expectations. You can restructure your organization, shifting responsibilities from one department or individual to another without producing headline stories in the business press all across the country. You can operate under the proverbial radar, introducing new products or variations on old ones without immediately generating competition from an industry leader. And you're closer to your customer—or, at least, you should be!

Let's assume for the moment that this is truly the case. You've put in place many of the practices we suggest to listen to your customers—or maybe you've even gone way beyond what we propose. You know what makes your customers tick, what they think, how they feel about your work, and even what moves them to do business with you. But an important question arises: do they share your company's values to an extent that will make them receptive to a social message that comes from you? By publicly acting on your company's values, will you attract customers—and employees—who agree with those values? We believe the answer is yes.

After all, your business is special. Your vision and mission are broader in scope than traditional business concerns. You want to make a difference. You operate in accordance with a set of values that sets you apart from your competitors.

Do your customers know that? Do you want them to know?

Within Social Venture Network, some companies go out of their way to "educate" their customers about the values that make them special. Others downplay or entirely ignore those values.

It's not about educating customers about your values. It's about operating your business based on your values and letting your customers determine what your values are.

For instance, Vatex America (highlighted in chapter 3) has adopted workplace policies that are extraordinarily generous. The extent to which founder and CEO Jerry Gorde has gone to share the power and perks of ownership with his employees is unusual. Yet (at the time we're writing this book) the home page of the company's Web site contains just a single sentence to hint at these policies and the values that animated them: "We are a proud employee owned company."

By contrast, take a look at the Web site for TS Designs (featured in chapter 7). The company is in a market niche very similar to that of Vatex. Yet its values are clearly written all over the company's home page. As the Web site states in so many words, "We believe a business can only prosper through a sustainable business model that adheres to the 3 P's, People, Profit and Planet."

You might also compare the approach taken by building products manufacturer Icestone, whose Web site makes clear that its mission is to "develop products that foster a sustainable environment," with the approach of another socially responsible business, Wild Planet Toys, a company whose mission appears nowhere on its Web site. The closest Wild Planet comes to sharing its values lies in the statement that leads a brief description in the "About Us" section: "We believe in the power of a child's imagination. Our toys and products encourage kids to be imaginative, creative and to explore the world around them."

Setting a policy for your company about whether to share your values with your customers will depend on a mix of pragmatic and emotional factors. You'll have to ask yourself whether your business's sales would be helped—or hurt—if you openly shared your vision, mission, and values. You'll also have to determine how important it is to you and your employees to show your true colors to the world.

In a niche market such as Warm Spirit's or even Seventh Generation's, it's reasonable to assume that at least some of the company's values are shared by its customers—and that values-driven marketing will be an advantage. That's one reason for the success these businesses have achieved. In fact, though, customers probably don't subscribe all that often to the values of the companies from which they buy. Some companies sell to a genuine mass market and find it wise to approach this question more cautiously. Take Worldwise, for example.

Worldwise
A Business Built on Feedback

You might say that listening to others is the very foundation of Worldwise, a leading brand of environmentally responsible consumer products. When cofounder Phil Genet found his daughters repeatedly coming home from grade school with environmentally conscious messages, the progressively minded fellow took his progeny seriously—so seriously that he decided to start a business based on products that would make the world a better and less polluted place. Genet partnered with Aaron Lamstein and Debra Lynn Dadd, and the three created Worldwise in 1990.

Having experimented over the years with a number of product categories, Worldwise now provides mainly pet products to the country's largest retailers, including Wal-Mart, Target, Safeway, and Walgreens. "Our idea from the beginning was to succeed in the mass market with products that truly served needs and provided environmental benefits at the same time," says Aaron Lamstein, president and CEO.

Selling more than 100,000 items a week in some 25,000 retail stores, Worldwise clearly has a diverse customer base. "The environmental benefits give us a little bit of an edge, but mainly we compete on the grounds that our products work as well as or better than the competition, look as good or finer, and cost the same or less," says Lamstein. Take the company's SmartyKat line for cats, for example. "We sell a cat scratcher that works better than carpeted posts because it truly prevents cats from clawing furniture," he explains. Made of postconsumer corrugated cardboard, the pad simulates the feel of tree bark, where cats would naturally scratch in the wild. Moreover, the pure catnip embedded inside attracts feline friends like a magnet. The scratcher clearly does its job at a reasonable cost—and an added bonus is the catnip is 100 percent certified organic, thereby exposing Fluffy to fewer toxins. And the entire pad can be thrown in the recycling bin when it's used up. "Carpeted scratch pads, by contrast, will stay in the landfill for a few thousand years," Lamstein says.

Worldwise's customers comprise retailers and consumers, and the company has dedicated itself to soliciting feedback from both from the get-go. "Our sales team is trained to ask retailers a lot of questions about what works and what doesn't and to find out where there are opportunities to better fulfill consumers' needs," says Lamstein. "If we hadn't done this from day one, we would have been out of business quickly. Not initially having had the buffer of much capital to rely on made us very feedback oriented. Now, such an approach is one of our greatest strategic weapons."

Building trust with consumers involves not only providing a superior product but also slightly underplaying product and environmental benefits on the packaging. "We underpromise and overperform, and that makes customers very happy," Lamstein explains. On the rare occasion when customers call to complain about a product, the Worldwise customer service team typically sends out not only a refund or replacement but also a related bonus gift. "People just jump up and down with excitement when you do that—we've got binders with letters to prove it," says Lamstein. "It's very inexpensive to exceed someone's expectations, and it creates a lot of goodwill."

The goodwill that Worldwise earns from its customers has helped to build its reputation as an extraordinary company, adding substantial value to the business. An analyst skilled in the techniques of evaluating goodwill may even be able to put a dollar figure on that value. Usually, most of us involved in small or midsized businesses have the opportunity to gain such precise information only when the time comes to evaluate the company for sale (or to put an ESOP in place). It would be a mistake, though, to ignore just how much a good reputation might be worth to you.

How much is your reputation worth?

As you may recall from chapter 1, a major study of the literature on the impact of socially responsible business policies and practices on companies' financial performance found a significant correlation between the two—and that this was the result of improved managerial performance and improved corporate reputation. This suggests that business executives who adopt a values-driven approach are actually better managers, presumably because the policies and practices they put in place reflect a broader and deeper understanding of today's business environment. The study also implies that these policies and practices enhance a company's reputation, giving it a leg up in recruiting top-notch staff, helping sustain high employee morale, and contributing toward a strong brand that attracts customers and helps keep them loyal. Some specialists refer to socially responsible business policies as "reputation insurance," regarding them as the steps a wise manager takes as a hedge against continuing changes in public attitudes toward the business sector.

If you're running a small business, it may be difficult to quantify the value of the "reputation insurance" you're buying as you build or steer your company along values-driven lines. However, you'll almost certainly find that the effort pays off, sometimes in surprising ways. Much the same is true of the efforts you take to build a mutually rewarding relationship with the community or communities where you do business.

That's the topic of the following chapter, "Staking Out Your Place in the Community."

Mobilizing Your Customers for Social Impact: A Checklist

Here's a list of suggested actions you can take to enlist your customers in joint efforts to improve the quality of life in your community.

Policy or practice	Adopt?
Use available space on your product packaging to highlight an issue that is of great concern to you and your employees. Invite customers to call a toll-free number set up by a nonprofit organization that will provide additional information and channel activists into productive activities.	☐
Produce a free customer newsletter, either online, in print, or both, and devote some of the space to statements about issues of concern—ideally including suggestions about practical steps readers can take to act on an issue.	☐
Offer free or at a discount other companies' products or services that convey a sense of caring to your customers and deliver a social benefit. For example, you might help a business owned by women or people of color to get off the ground by introducing your customer base to its products or services.	☐
Either on your own or using the services of a public relations agency, seek to have articles or interviews placed about your work in trade publications, using as a publicity hook your company's outspokenness on a controversial issue.	☐
Either on your own or using the services of a public relations agency, place an occasional feature story about your company's active involvement in public policy issues in a local newspaper or magazine or on radio or television.	☐
Prepare inserts on issues of concern to place in your packages or invoices, ideally including explicit information about how readers can take action to support the position you advocate.	☐
Offer tours of your plant or offices to introduce customers to the values that drive your business and the policies and practices that you've put in place. Use the opportunity to urge them to participate in an advocacy campaign in which your company is involved. Distribute take-home materials that enable them to take action on that campaign.	☐

Policy or practice	Adopt?
Participate in community events by setting up exhibits or information tables at which you can distribute literature on issues that matter to you as well as to inform visitors about your company's products or services.	☐
Make philanthropic contributions to nonprofits that embody the values you champion and that take action on the issues that represent your highest priorities.	☐

6

Staking out your place in the community

For almost any retail business, location is critical. A shop on a side street may languish while one on the corner thrives. But anyone in business who has thought through the implications of siting a business is well aware that its location has a great many consequences, good or bad:

- Opening up a plant in a neighborhood of high unemployment may provide a ready source of willing labor.

- An office or plant with access to good public transportation may lower the costs of working there, thus reducing upward pressure on wages or salaries.

- Having an office in a high-crime area may dampen recruitment and make late-evening projects dangerous.

- Setting up shop at home may disrupt family routines, raise tempers, and reduce productivity.

- Locating in an office park near companies in related businesses may open up possibilities for productive strategic alliances and cross-fertilization.

- Placing a research facility near the campus of a major university may help attract world-class talent.

Location, location, location

However, pragmatic considerations such as these touch on only a part of the question. Just as a dialogue characterizes the relationship between a company and its customers, an ongoing, two-way "conversation" occurs between a business and the surrounding community. At a minimum, a company's employees are likely to visit local shops and restaurants even if they don't live nearby. Local residents may covet jobs at the company, whether or not they are qualified. Local governments usually charge business taxes. Community-based nonprofit organizations may seek donations from the company and its employees. The chamber of commerce, the Rotary Club, and other local institutions will probably look to the company or its principal as a potential member. How you handle these relationships—how you manage the dialogue with the community or communities where you do business—can have significant influence on how smoothly your company operates.

As a values-driven businessperson, though, you may wish to play an active role, not just respond passively to inquiries and requests. If you want to make a significant difference in your community, perhaps you'll emulate the White Dog Cafe, one of the nation's most outstanding examples of a business that operates by and for its community.

White Dog Cafe
Good Food as a Lure for Activism

The White Dog Cafe, founded in 1983, is a restaurant in Philadelphia that features foods from local organic family farms. It also serves as a center for social activism, sponsoring numerous programs and events at its 200-seat premises throughout the year. Characterized by food, fun, and the promotion of social justice, it is an apt landmark in a city named for "brotherly love."

With gross revenues of $5 million a year, the White Dog Cafe hands over 20 percent of its profits to its own White Dog Cafe Foundation and to other local nonprofit organizations. The foundation works to build a local living economy in the region, both in terms of community life and natural life. Its Fair Food project, for example, provides consulting and print guides for other restaurants, wholesalers, and consumers on how to buy products from local farmers, including meats from humane animal farms. The project sponsors an annual "Buy Local" week, which includes farm tours, produce-tasting events, and cooking demonstrations all aimed at educating the public about the importance of supporting family farms. It also runs the Fair Food Farmstand in the Reading Terminal Market, the only stand in the market that buys 100 percent of its meat from local farmers with cruelty-free practices. And Fair Food administers grants to help local pig farmers convert from indoor to outdoor farming and expand their heritage breeds.

The foundation's Sustainable Business Network also helps support, connect, and promote independent, locally owned businesses, including renewable-energy independent retailers, recycling companies, and other enterprises necessary for creating a sustainable local economy. The program hosts educational events every month on sustainable-business topics, including the importance of using renewable energy and buying goods and services locally.

"Our efforts are all about building an economy that benefits our own community," says Judy Wicks, White Dog's founder and owner. "We encourage people to switch from buying at large chain stores, which just sap the capital out of Philadelphia, to supporting locally owned businesses that keep capital circulating within our region. We also encourage them to divest from the stock market and invest in the local reinvestment fund that loans money to local businesses, farms, and renewable energy companies."

The cafe itself, staffed by 100 dedicated employees, also hosts a whirlwind of nonstop activities, including monthly community service days that bring people into the community to plant gardens and trees, build affordable houses for Habitat for Humanity, or coordinate clothing drives for women coming off welfare. The cafe partners with local nonprofits to host a variety of local tours for customers, educating them about the lives of inner-city children; the work of environmental groups in areas such as water conservation, recycling, solar energy, and other issues; and local arts and garden efforts. The cafe's "sister restaurant" project helps support minority-owned restaurants in the inner city with resources, information, publicity, and a stream of customers.

The cafe is also frequently the site of cultural celebrations and dances, as well as a progressive film and educational series featuring noted speakers on topics such as the AIDS epidemic, the drug war, and humanitarian crises around the world. The cafe's annual Thanksgiving bash acknowledges with gratitude the many foods in our diet contributed by Native Americans, honors members of the local Lenape Nation, and features a speaker on contemporary Native American issues. A yearly Martin Luther King dinner celebrates the memory of the slain leader. And a Gandhi breakfast reinforces the principles of nonviolence promoted by the famous Indian visionary. Local members of the community also share their personal experiences with immigration, incarceration, war, and other matters on storytelling evenings. The restaurant also gives away small grants to help local community groups in their efforts and mentors inner-city high school students who are interested in going into the restaurant business.

"I use good food to lure innocent customers into social activism," quips Wicks. "I see the restaurant basically as a vehicle for social change. It's obvious to me that people are not just hungry for food, they're hungry for meaning and for the opportunity to discuss issues they care about as part of a community."

Judy Wicks and the White Dog Cafe have earned a considerable share of fame for their extraordinarily expansive view of community. Another SVN-affiliated company that has gained widespread attention is Greyston Bakery, which takes a very different approach to its own, very different community.

Greyston Bakery
A Very Different Community

Greyston Bakery was founded in 1982 by Zen Buddhist priest Bernie Glassman, and it shows. The enterprise is focused on taking a compassionate view toward society's least fortunate members—those who lack job skills or legal documentation, substance abusers, people who have been incarcerated, welfare mothers, and those who are homeless or who have AIDS. The bakery provides them with jobs and the support they need to turn their lives around. These citizens, located specifically in the Yonkers area of New York where the bakery has its home, are employed to produce the ubiquitous brownies and cakes used as inclusions in ice cream for Ben & Jerry's, Häagen-Dazs, Good Humor, Cumberland Farms, and Stonyfield Farm, as well as wholesale cakes for distribution to restaurants and cafes. This year, the bakery expects to earn $6.3 million in revenues. It has consistently been profitable.

Most of the bakery's seventy employees are taken on through open hiring: the first person to apply for an entry-level position gets the job. Employees are subsequently provided with training and a work environment in which expectations are made clear. "This gives them a greater chance of developing the skills and discipline they need to hold down a job," says Julius Walls, the bakery's president and CEO. "We make efforts to address our workers and their issues with consciousness.

"As we've helped people move onto a path of a greater self-sufficiency," he adds, "we've realized that they—and the broader community—have life needs that must be taken care of in order for them to be successful, as well." As a result, the Greyston Foundation, which was formed in the mid-1990s, now supports some 1,200 families, only a small percentage of whom work at Greyston. The foundation's outreach includes 224 units of affordable housing in the greater New York area; child-care facilities; a youth program for young people sixteen to twenty-one who are no longer participating in the school system; after-school programs for children; job skill building and placement programs; and a health-care facility that provides acute and primary care specializing in HIV/AIDS as well as alternative health treatments, counseling, and crisis management. The bakery donates $200,000 to $400,000 each year to the foundation's efforts.

Greyston boasts numerous success stories—employees who have taken advantage of the opportunities available to them through the bakery to get their lives in order, develop professional and life skills, and move on to bigger and better things. Mothers on welfare have developed vibrant careers, fathers who had been assumed to be deadbeat dads have been able to support their children, drug addicts have gotten clean, and former prisoners have turned their lives around and become productive citizens. "If all businesses operated responsibly, there would be no need to talk of the extra work of 'giving back to the community,'" says Walls. "It would just be a natural extension of what we do daily."

If Greyston's recipe of direct action to right social wrongs and or the White Dog's extensive menu of community-involvement projects seem a little rich for your taste, you might consider a gradual approach. Launching a couple of projects per year will add up to an impressive array of activities faster than you might realize. You're likely to find, as you pursue this course, that you get a whole lot in return.

How to give something back and get a lot in return

Are you familiar with the old adage "What goes around, comes around"? That's a convenient way to look at what happens—over time—as you steer your company into deeper and deeper involvement in the community or communities where you do business. Here are just a few of the significant benefits that may help strengthen your business—and enrich your life:

- Your employees' morale will rise. Even if they take part in community activities where your office or plant is located rather than in the nearby town where they live, your co-workers will be gratified by an opportunity to add meaning to the efforts they make to build your business.

- You'll find that the word-of-mouth buzz about your company is gathering momentum. You may find it easier to attract the skilled and highly motivated new employees you want.

- If you have customers or clients in your local community, you'll find the company's reputation is improving among them. You can expect greater customer loyalty and personal referrals for new business.

- Staking out your place as a community-oriented business will attract the attention of civic leaders in all fields, widening the access you have to the community's decision makers and smoothing the way in the event that questions arise about zoning or other permits.

- As your company's reputation for community-mindedness grows, you'll find it easier to get to know like-minded business leaders. This will open up opportunities to exchange ideas and experiences, expanding the breadth of your horizon and suggesting new ideas for you and your employees to consider.

Community involvement comes in many varieties. But the most familiar and most common means to express a company's values in its community is old-fashioned philanthropy. However, even that practice has lots of room for creativity, as the story of Eileen Fisher's twentieth anniversary grant-making program shows so clearly.

Eileen Fisher
A Very Special Celebration

Amy Hall of Eileen Fisher says, "2004 marked our twentieth anniversary and we wanted to do more than just throw a big party. We wanted to celebrate this event at all levels of the company because we recognized that it was the entire Eileen Fisher family—employees, vendors, suppliers, community partners, sales accounts, etcetera—that led to our success over the years."

To celebrate the anniversary, the company created a special one-time grant program (over and above its annual grant-making program), offering five grants of $20,000 each. Grants were earmarked for four nonprofit issue areas (all supporting women), with the fifth to go to a woman-owned *for-profit* business. This enabled Eileen Fisher to do something both meaningful and symbolic to include its community in the celebration of an important company milestone.

The grant program led to a big PR story, positively impacting the company's brand image, and helped to deepen its community ties.

The idea for this special grant-making initiative came from the company's staff. "The leadership of the company asked all employees to suggest ways to celebrate the twentieth anniversary within their own work areas," explains Hall. "The Social Consciousness Department, which manages the company's community outreach, among other things, suggested offering the grants through a competition." The idea was immediately approved.

The department then took the following steps: (1) determined five grant areas, four for nonprofit organizations addressing specific women's issues and one for a for-profit woman-owned business; (2) created guidelines for the grant review process; (3) announced the grant competition on the company Web site and through e-mail; (4) received hundreds of applications, which staff sorted and distributed among Donations Committee members for review; (5) arranged site visits, conference calls, or in-person meetings with five finalists in each grant category; (6) made the decision three months after issuing the announcement; (7) invited all grantees (two representatives from each organization) to the corporate headquarters, all expenses paid, for a grant award lunch at Fisher's house; and (8) got publicity in local and regional media.

"The most significant result was simply the goodwill generated among the grantees and within their own communities, where they each sought substantial publicity," adds Hall. "The monetary value of the grants less important than the time and energy we spent in getting to know each grantee."

One of the principal factors was the grantee's own culture and how it resonated with the company's.

"The principal obstacle we faced," Hall explains, "was that we had never before offered a competitive grant. We had to create the process from scratch—and in a way that reflected the Eileen Fisher corporate culture—and complete the entire grant process in a very short period of time with employee volunteers only. Hence our second obstacle: time.

"While employees were able to work on this on company time, they still were also getting their 'regular work' done, so in effect, people on the committee were donating a significant amount of their own time to the effort. In some cases, people were being asked to take extra hours—days, even—out of their schedule to conduct site visits, meet with their fellow committee members, and review proposals. It was exhausting work. But it was clear that this was a company priority, and no one felt uneasy about committing as much time as was necessary to do this properly."

In designing this one-time grant award program—linked to a specific corporate anniversary or milestone—Eileen Fisher staff discovered that a for-profit woman-owned business grant was extremely rare and that the company was truly breaking new ground by offering such grants. Moreover, the moral support offered to grantees by company staff was just as important as the dollar amount.

"What we learned from this process," says Hall, "is that there are endless ways that our peers could make a positive impact in their communities without spending a great deal of money. In fact, we hope that other businesses will think about offering grants to small businesses themselves—especially those that are aligned with their values. What better way to advance the cause of socially responsible business than to give a leg up to a like-minded fledgling enterprise?"

For Eileen Fisher, a profitable midsized company with more than 400 employees and sales now approaching $200 million, the resources for philanthropy are plentiful. At other companies, that isn't often the case. Also, many traditional companies have a pronounced tendency to turn to philanthropy as an inexpensive way to avoid taking more meaningful steps to engage the company and its employees in the life of the community.

Is philanthropy the answer?

Philanthropy is a wonderful thing. When you give away money to a cause you hold dear, you feel terrific, knowing that you've helped others act on the values that give your life meaning. Philanthropy is a major force in American life, diverting more than $1 out of every $50 generated by this most massive economy on the planet to the organizations and institutions that constitute the nonprofit sector. Of the nearly $250 billion estimated to have been contributed voluntarily by Americans in 2004, some $12 billion, or 4.8 percent, came from corporations. The impact in improving the quality of life in our country, though hard to measure, was undoubtedly significant.

But is philanthropy enough from the perspective of a values-driven business? The answer is obviously no.

Ben & Jerry's engaged in philanthropy, diverting 7.5 percent of its pretax net profit to the Ben & Jerry's Foundation. But Ben and Jerry always felt that the company's most meaningful and powerful impact on society came from the many ways it integrated social concerns into its day-to-day business activities. Doing so helps make socially beneficial activism sustainable, replicable, and scalable. There's a limit to how much money you can give away, but there's no limit to how much you can integrate a concern for the community into the way you do business. It was this point of view that led Ben & Jerry's to

- Invest in credit unions and low-income housing

- Use chlorine-free paper for its packaging

- Generate members for the Children's Defense Fund by pre-senting information about the organization and its work on its packages

- Help endangered family farms stay in business by buying all its cream and milk from them

- Reduce threats to public health by using only dairy products free of bovine growth hormone

- Support the preservation of the rainforest by creating a fla-vor called Rainforest Crunch, which used Brazil nuts to demonstrate that the rainforest was as profitable when sus-tainably harvested as when it was cut down and turned into cattle ranches

Philanthrophy also has drawbacks. For starters, you can get into the game only if you have the price of admission. You can't give away what you don't have. And you'll gain relatively little if you make all the decisions yourself. A philanthropic program in the workplace tends to be more effective if the employees par-ticipate in making decisions about where the money will go.

By including staff in the decision-making process, many a company has successfully organized a philanthropic program that has strengthened its position in the community, provided a great sense of satisfaction to employees and management alike, and broadened its social impact by enabling resourceful non-profit organizations to expand their work. Mal Warwick & Associates is one such company.

Mal Warwick & Associates
Giving Back to the Community

Every quarter, Mal Warwick & Associates sets aside 10 percent of its pretax profits in its Philanthropic Fund to support causes and organizations selected by employees. The money is distributed in two ways: through two to one contributions to match those employees give to nonprofit organizations of their choice and through direct contributions to local nonprofit organizations dedicated to promoting social change in the company's local community, chiefly through the Berkeley Community Fund, the town's innovative community foundation.

Conceptually, the process is simple. Once the annual fund amount is set, the total is divided by the number of employees (with a proportionally smaller amount allocated to part-time employees). Employees select the charities they want to support. Employees may submit proof to the accounting staff of charitable contributions made to their chosen charities during the prior year and thus eligible for matching. Employee contributions will be matched up to their pro-rata share of the fund. Funds not used to match employee contributions go into a fund to support local nonprofits.

The Philanthropic Fund serves three ends: to promote philanthropy, which is one aspect of the company's mission; to provide a benefit to employees that many of them value highly; and to promote social change in the company's backyard.

The company's policy of supporting community nonprofits arose in the mid-1990s when, as a result of ideas acquired through attendance at SVN conferences, Mal, then CEO, sought advice from the company's staff and board about new employee benefits the firm might offer. Several employees suggested ideas along the lines of what became the Philanthropic Fund. The board of directors then adopted the policy.

Over the years, employee participation in the philanthropic program has varied from 50 percent to 75 percent, largely varying with economic conditions. As many as 100 nonprofit organizations, including a number of the firm's clients (all nonprofits), have received contributions in any given year through the program. A half-dozen outstanding Berkeley nonprofits have regularly received significant cash gifts each year since the program's inception in 1997.

The Philanthropic Fund was not universally welcomed at first at Mal Warwick & Associates. Several board members were initially skeptical that the company could afford to set aside 10 percent of its pretax net profits for philanthropy. The CFO and the company's consulting accountant argued—unsuccessfully—that the percentage should be set at a lower level. But the sentiment to make a bold statement of community involvement prevailed.

For the program's tax-deductible status to be maintained, the charities themselves must qualify as tax-exempt nonprofit organizations under Section 501(c)(3) of the Internal Revenue Code. Other than that, Mal Warwick & Associates imposes no restrictions on the choice of eligible nonprofits. However, on another company, the owner or manager needs to think carefully whether any additional restrictions should be imposed on the groups to be supported. For example, the owner may find that some staff members elect to support causes she wouldn't want to back.

An additional issue arises when deciding what to do with funds not used to meet matching requirements. At Mal Warwick & Associates, the remainder is spent on local charities promoting social change. Because funds are used locally, these grants are channeled not toward specific profits or programs but toward "core support," which is often difficult for nonprofit organizations to secure from foundations or major donors.

Naturally, this program requires both money and time—time largely on the part of the company's accounting department, which must manage a program involving hundreds of pieces of paper and nearly a hundred checks every year. The money has to come from profits. Fortunately, the company has been consistently profitable since the program's inception in 1997.

At Mal Warwick & Associates, the company's philanthropic program is shaped by its commitment to social change. At Immaculate Baking, another SVN-affiliated company, a much more specific concern plays the central role.

Immaculate Baking
Cookies for the Arts

When Scott Blackwell founded Immaculate Baking Company in his garage in Flat Rock, North Carolina, in 1995, he had two missions: to produce a pure, organic cookie with a fun twist and to give back. At first, baking no-skimp cookies in flavors such as lemon white chocolate, pumpkin ginger, and triple chocolate and coming up with innovations like Mojos chocolate-dipped biscotti bites proved easier than finding a way to help the community. But by following his other passion—collecting folk art primarily from the American Southeast—he hit upon the perfect idea.

"I was obsessed not only with the art but with the people producing it, who were mostly poor, uneducated, and oppressed people living in squalor," says the CEO and president. Impressed with the raw creativity, color, and vibrancy of their work, Blackwell started buying the rights from artists to reproduce images of their art on Immaculate Baking's cookie packages—a practice he continues today.

But Blackwell felt he wasn't doing enough, particularly when he'd run into artists like Leonard Jones, a middle-aged

African-American man living in the kind of metal storage building you can buy at Home Depot. "It was the middle of winter and freezing out, and I found him at his place and thought, I can't leave here today without helping him," Blackwell says. "Here was an artist who was selling work to galleries and collectors all over the country and yet didn't have a decent place to live. That's when the idea of how I could do more struck me." Blackwell helped Jones find more decent living quarters that day and agreed to have Immaculate Baking pay for two years of his rent. That small gesture led to the creation of the Folk Artists Foundation (FAF) in 1999, which channels a percentage of company profits to help support local artists.

Still feeling frustrated by his ability to help only a few people at a time with small grants and donated food and clothing, however, Blackwell got the idea to bake a 40,000-pound cookie, sell pieces of it, and put the money into the foundation. Through the resulting media exposure, Blackwell has received funding from the National Endowment for the Arts, other organizations, and private citizens to expand the work of FAF. The nonprofit has since provided opportunities for local artists to earn money by participating in traveling exhibits and teaching art to at-risk children. FAF will soon build a workshop and gallery space where folk artists can live, teach, and show and sell their work. Blackwell himself completed a documentary on folk artists, *All Rendered Truth,* which is currently meeting with great success on the film festival circuit.

Meanwhile, Immaculate Baking, whose cookies are widely distributed throughout natural foods grocery chains, continues to give money to the nonprofit in both fat years and lean. The company, now grown to a staff of fifteen, has also sponsored several kids' cookie bakes as fund-raisers for other nonprofit organizations benefiting children around the country. "I do this because it teaches me something new about life every day," says Blackwell. "I'm not a Buddhist, but I do believe in karma. When you die, you can't take your money with you, but what you can take is what you've done for your soul. That's the principle I live by."

In some cases, such as at Immaculate Baking, Give Something Back (chapter 2), and Pura Vida Coffee (chapter 4), the philanthropic impulse itself led to the establishment of the company. In many others, philanthropy is one of a great many factors through which a business expresses its values. We see similar diversity among values-driven companies when it comes to environmental policies and practices, which are the subject of the next chapter.

Digging Deeper into Your Community: A Checklist

This checklist suggests a number of ways you can use your business as a launching pad for activities that will benefit your community while raising your employees' morale and improving your company's reputation.

Policy or practice	Adopt?
Set up a company-wide volunteer program to help build homes for Habitat for Humanity, take part in an environmental cleanup at a stream or beach, or work in some other constructive way with a local nonprofit organization. (Not everyone will participate, but many will. Either way, it's a benefit.)	☐
Consider whether your company might "adopt" a nonprofit or a fledgling minority- or woman-owned business through cash contributions or an investment, mentoring, and sharing of resources, perhaps including unused office space, office equipment, and furniture.	☐
Talk to your employees—and to the appropriate local authorities—about the possibility of holding a block party for all your neighbors.	☐

Policy or practice	Adopt?
Set up a philanthropic matching-gift program that will match employee contributions to charity at least one to one. If necessary, set a limit on the total donations any employee may submit for matching.	☐
Contact your local community foundation (if there is one). Determine whether gifts to the foundation could be a viable alternative to selecting individual nonprofits to receive the company's support.	☐
Hold a staff meeting to discuss philanthropy with your employees. Ask for ideas and opinions about different ways to organize a philanthropic program for your company.	☐
Sponsor a forum for local companies to discuss the advantages of values-driven business.	☐
Hold an open house for the community. If it's appropriate, set up tours of your plant on a regular schedule and invite all comers to learn about your work.	☐
Talk to the principal of the local high school. Volunteer to host a session for students to learn about your company's work—and the world of work in general.	☐
Once a month, invite a leading local nonprofit organization to speak briefly at an employee staff meeting to familiarize you and your coworkers with its work. If you have the space, open these meetings to your customers.	☐
When possible, locate your company's operations in underserved communities to generate employment and job training opportunities.	☐
Focus on one critical community problem and use your company's financial and political influence to create change.	☐
Host an annual donations celebration, honoring the nonprofit groups your company supports.	☐

7

Leaving a lighter footprint on the planet

Let's face it. Your company probably isn't clubbing furry little animals to death or dumping millions of gallons of toxic waste into the river that runs through town. Unless you're manufacturing something that uses carcinogenic chemicals, creating a Superfund site in your backyard, or actively defying environmental regulations, you may feel that your footprint on the planet isn't heavy.

Well, guess again. Think about how much you travel (including commuting), about how much energy you and your company use, about the materials in your building, about how much paper is consumed in your work, about the food you eat and the water you use. Simply living and doing business in twenty-first-century America practically ensures that every one of us devours an immoderate share of the earth's resources. According to Mathis Wackernagel, widely regarded as one of the world's leading thinkers on environmental impact, if every person on the earth consumed at the level of the average American, we'd need three to five more planets to supply us.[3] Just for example, Paul Hawken estimates it takes about 40,000 pounds of materials just to make a 4-pound laptop computer.[4]

Assessing your company's environmental impact

In any case, society (and government) might look on you a little differently in another part of the world—in many European countries, for example, where environmental regulations tend to be much more stringent than in North America. You might learn, for example, that complying with the law would require you to reengineer your production, packaging, and distribution systems. Even if the law didn't require such thoroughgoing changes, consumers might.

Here in the United States, pioneering companies—like those profiled in this chapter—are setting the standards. When you become acquainted with the policies and practices they've put in place, you'll see that your company affects the quality of the environment in a surprising number of ways. Their efforts go leagues beyond recycling programs:

- The means of transportation you and your employees use to get to work may be generating far more pollution and using far more energy than anything you do in the workplace.

- The plastic components in your packaging may be burdening landfills and squandering precious petroleum resources.

- Your computers, printers, and other office equipment may be wasting large amounts of energy—not to mention the old refrigerator in your office kitchen.

- Old plumbing or electrical fixtures could be frittering away significant amounts of water or electricity—and costing you extra in the process.

- The old windows and window frames in your plant may be leaking heat in the winter and admitting it in the summer, resulting in the overuse of energy and the raising of your heating and air-conditioning bills.

- The energy you use, if it comes from fossil fuels, is contributing to global climate changes.

The circumstances at your company are unique, of course. Perhaps none of these conditions apply to you. Chances are, however, if you haven't looked into these questions, it would make good sense for you to undertake an *environmental audit* and an *energy audit*. In some places, state or local governments offer one or another of these as a service. Occasionally, the power company conducts free energy audits to encourage energy conservation and reduce pressure to build expensive new power plants. In addition, a substantial number of companies offer environmental or energy audits as a commercial service. (To locate such companies, you might start by consulting an environmental organization in your community or by searching the Internet.)

Ben & Jerry's, which was founded in 1978, was one of the first companies in the nation to undertake a systematic environmental audit. The company formed an in-house "green team" to examine every aspect of its operations to learn how the business could become environmentally friendlier. One of the results was a recycling program, one of the first in the country at a business. Another outcome was the discovery that the production of the chlorine bleach used in Ben & Jerry's packaging created dioxins, one of the most toxic substances known to humankind. So Ben & Jerry's became the first company selling ice cream in pints to stop packaging them in containers produced using chlorine bleach.

Much later in its history, Mal Warwick & Associates conducted an intensive environmental audit and a later, separate energy audit. The outcome was dramatic. Based on recommendations from the consultant who conducted the environmental audit, the company

- Significantly reduced health risks to employees from ozone and electromagnetic radiation
- Increased the efficiency of its already extensive recycling program
- Introduced incentives for employees to ride bikes or take public transportation to work
- Systematically reached out to its suppliers to review their own environmentally significant practices
- Drew up a written Environmental Policy Statement to guide future management decision making.

Later, the energy audit led the firm to change lighting and plumbing fixtures and take other steps to conserve resources that resulted in significant cost savings. The net impact of all these changes was improved workplace morale, less pollution, more efficient resource use—and higher profits!

Sometimes you make more money by making environmentally friendly decisions. Sometimes it costs money. In the end, the financial impact probably balances out, but the net effect will be that everyone benefits: your employees, your customers, and the community as well as the environment. For example, Ben & Jerry's replaced all its motors with energy-efficient models and was able to save money as a result. Another company may make the decision to buy only electricity generated by wind power. In today's market, that would probably cost it money. Of course, benefits may result from doing so, anyway. For example, that move might appeal to customers and lead to increased sales. But it would be naïve to make the decision with that expectation.

For Ben & Jerry's and Mal Warwick & Associates, environmental impact was one among many values-driven concerns. However, a substantial number of companies all across the country are based primarily on a quest for sustainability.

The concept of sustainability is far broader than the question of environmental impact. The United Nations defines sustainability as meeting the needs of the present generation without compromising the ability of future generations to meet their needs.[5] In practical, down-to-business terms, sustainability then boils down to honoring the triple bottom line of people, planet, and profits. TS Designs is one firm that aspires to meet that definition.

TS Designs
Seeking Sustainability

TS Designs, based in Burlington, North Carolina, manufactures and sells the highest quality, most sustainable, printed apparel. To TS Designs, "sustainable" means domestically made, produced with organic cotton, and printed with REHANCE, an environmentally friendly ink system the company developed and patented.

The company, founded in 1977 by Tom Sineath, originally printed T-shirts for big brands such as Nike, the Gap, and Tommy Hilfiger, but when the North American Free Trade Agreement went into effect twelve years ago and these corporations began outsourcing their production more cheaply overseas, TS Designs literally had to switch gears to survive. The company decided to stay in the business but change its course, focusing on its core value of sustainability. Now, rather than buying and printing T-shirts made offshore, the company works with suppliers from the organic cotton yarn phase all the way to the finished product.

"Instead of selling a 50-cent print on a Nike T-shirt, we're now selling an $8 T-shirt to Whole Foods," says Eric Henry, company president. "People said it couldn't be profitable, but we're proving them wrong."

Part of TS Designs' competitive edge comes from the fact that purveyors appreciate not only that the shirts are made of organic cotton but that they are printed using the company's patented REHANCE process, a print and dye operation that uses low-impact dyes and avoids the toxic chemicals usually associated with apparel printing. They also like TS Designs' sustainable business philosophy. "If you go outside your market for products or services that your market could supply, then that's not sustainable," says Henry. Last year, the company started making organic cotton T-shirts right in North Carolina, a state that has lost thousands of apparel jobs. "In four to five years we hope to be growing organic cotton here," he says.

The company continually works to reduce its consumption of nonrenewable resources, too. "Electricity in North Carolina is some of the cheapest in the country, produced mostly by coal-powered plants, but the price reflects only today's cost," says Henry. "It doesn't measure the long-term costs of acid rain, ozone depletion, mercury poisoning, and other polluting effects from the burning of coal to produce that electricity." To conserve, TS Designs implemented a high-technology lighting system and added switches to allow various areas of its operations to be turned on and off according to need. The company installed a two-kilowatt solar array in front of its building, as well. "The energy generated in this way costs us a lot more per kilowatt, but considering the devastation to the environment that more cheaply produced electricity creates, it's worth it to us," Henry says. "Our goal is to eventually be functioning 100 percent on renewable energy."

TS Designs contributes to the nonprofit organization NC Green Power, which means it pays an extra charge per kilowatt on its regular monthly utility bill. Utility companies use those monies to replace coal-burning technologies with renewable technologies such as solar and wind.

The company has also instituted another measure to lessen its imprint on the environment: it collects water off its ice machines, compressors, and air conditioners—which amounts to about 250 gallons per day—and uses it to flush toilets. "Even though water is plentiful here, we believe we have a responsibility to preserve it for the planet," says Henry.

The company's building, located on about four acres, is landscaped to have a low impact on the surrounding ecosystem, as well. "Typically, offices around here cut down most of their trees and put down a lawn, but we're believers in the permaculture model," says Henry. The company has preserved or planted hundreds of new trees, put in wildflowers and plants local to the region, created walking paths, and established a communal organic garden. "We end up saving thousands of dollars a year on mowing costs. And because the trees give us shade, we save on air conditioning bills, too. It's really a no-brainer," Henry says.

The company is conscious of its environmental impact even in small ways. In its visitor lounge, for example, only free-trade coffee is served. Polystyrene cups and individually wrapped sweetener packets have been replaced with ceramic mugs and a good old metal spoon.

"It's been a difficult road, but we're now starting to see the benefits of integrating the three Ps—people, planet, and profits—into our business," says Henry.

Of the many ways that TS Designs is moving toward sustainability, it may be that the most significant lies in its use of organic cotton. The apparel industry's use of cotton has enormous environmental impact. Cotton represents about 25 percent of the total use of pesticides in this county. Intuitively, one might think that's fine because no one eats cotton, but that's wrong. Cottonseed oil, which ultimately absorbs most of the pesticides, is one of the most frequently used oils for packaged fried foods and fryers in restaurants. So the widespread use of nonorganic cotton in clothing has created a potentially major public health risk. Even worse, the extensive use of pesticides in growing cotton pollutes water supplies, the air, and ultimately the rain.

In response to such growing risks around the world, a Swedish physician and cancer researcher, Karl-Henrik Robert, developed an approach to planetary sustainability called the Natural Step. After twenty-one drafts of a paper outlining a comprehensive process that any organization could put to work, Dr. Robert achieved consensus from fifty leading Swedish scientists and gained the backing of the king of Sweden.

The Natural Step Framework

According to Terry Gips, president of the Alliance for Sustainability and an independent Natural Step Framework advocate and trainer, the Natural Step Framework is based on four sustainability principles or system conditions. He explains:

1. "To avoid systematically increasing concentrations of substances extracted from the earth's crust, we need to use renewable energy and nontoxic, reusable materials to avoid the spread of hazardous mined metals and pollutants."

2. "Because Nature must not be subject to systematically increasing concentrations of substances produced by society, we need to use safe, biodegradable substances that do not cause the spread of toxins in the environment."

3. "To avoid subjecting Nature to degradation by physical means, we need to protect our soils, water, and air, or we won't be able to eat, drink, or breathe."

4. "To meet basic human needs worldwide, we can use less stuff and save money while meeting the needs of every human on this planet."

Widespread adoption of the Natural Step Framework in Sweden has yielded impressive results. More than sixty corporations in Sweden have implemented the framework, including the world's largest manufacturers of appliances (Electrolux) and furniture (Ikea), OK Petroleum, Swedish Railways, three major supermarket chains, the largest hotel chain (Scandic), and McDonald's. The Natural Step was brought to the United States by author Paul Hawken and organizational learning professor Peter Senge in the early 1990s. It has now been utilized by many U.S. corporations, nonprofit organizations, and government agencies.

The Natural Step Framework offers a methodical, down-to-earth method of addressing some of the most daunting environmental and social challenges humanity faces, as well as opportunities for saving money, improving performance, and creating a shared, inspiring vision. Check it out online.

Whatever your values and your priorities, you can't help noticing that, in the long run, the environmental damage humankind has created may trump every other problem on the horizon. A comprehensive, values-driven approach to business is incomplete without taking steps to lessen that damage and ensure that the earth remains livable for our children and our children's children. Sadly, to cite just one aspect of the damage, the world's industry has polluted the earth's air and water—and, far too often, our bodies, as well—with an unimaginably diverse array of toxic substances. Many of these chemicals arise from the landfills we have created in the vicinity of our cities. Some companies committed to sustainability make their major contribution by reducing the flow of garbage to landfills. Recycline is a brilliant example.

Recycline
"A Toothbrush Is a Beginning"

If you wonder where all of those recycled yogurt containers end up, you may find the answer in Recycline toothbrushes, razors, tongue cleaners, and now even cutlery and toothpicks. Founded in 1996 and located in Waltham, Massachusetts, Recyline is one example of a company that is creating a second life for our plastic junk.

"I founded the company in the mid-1990s based on the fact that more and more people were recycling and wanting products made out of recycled material, but there wasn't enough demand in the marketplace to make recycling worthwhile," says president and CEO Eric Hudson. Recycline goods, sold under the Preserve brand, are helping to create and expand the market for recycled plastics, in particular, by using computer wafer chip containers, ketchup bottles, and dairy containers such as Stonyfield Farm yogurt cups for their raw source material.

The company evaluates its environmental imprint in every action it takes. Requiring its manufacturing vendors to use recycled plastics to produce its products is its most important step. This reduces America's demand for crude oil and natural gas—from which virgin plastic is produced—as well as the environmental disruption caused by the exploration, mining, and transportation of these precious resources. It also lessens air pollution.

Then there's the sourcing of colors. For this, the company has chosen to use zinc rather than titanium dioxide because mining zinc involves a less environmentally intrusive process. The firm similarly switched from talc to calcium carbonate because some of its customers did not want talc anywhere near their mouths for health reasons and because calcium carbonate is a renewable resource. Even the company's packaging has met with scrutiny: Recycline is researching a switch to recycled PET plastic (the kind that sports the "1" symbol) rather than the cellulose proprionate that it currently uses. While the latter is made from sustainably forested wood, it requires excessive bleaching processes to produce.

For Hudson, using recycled plastic as source material is not only earth-smart, it also happens to be budget-smart. "At the current price of oil and gas, we save almost 20 cents a pound on recycled versus virgin sourced plastic. That's raising some heads in the industry," he says. "The more we can introduce other companies to the idea that using recycled materials results in cost savings, the more we can create demand for them."

Hudson offers a few words of advice to other business leaders concerned with leaving a lighter footprint on the planet. "Take one step at a time," he says. "Don't try to do too much all at once, or you'll be less likely to start. Be glad for your small accomplishments, even if you're not perfect yet. If everyone made just moderate efforts, we'd be well on our road to improving our Earth-harming ways. A toothbrush is a small thing, but it's a beginning."

Like Recycline and TS Designs, New Leaf Paper has also set out on the path of sustainability. With a single-minded focus on recycled paper, the company is bringing change to a traditional industry that is often cited for the damage it does to the environment.

New Leaf Paper
"Paper with a Past and a Future"

New Leaf Paper, headquartered in San Francisco, develops and distributes environmentally sound printing and office paper throughout North America. The company expects to generate close to $19 million in revenues in 2005—up significantly from $1 million in 1998, its first year of operation. Winning the bid to be the paper source for the Harry Potter book series and gaining a presence at Kinko's has certainly contributed to the rise. "We're self-funded and have been able to manage rapid growth and low margins without taking in venture capital," says president and founder Jeff Mendelsohn. "We aim to drive the entire paper industry toward sustainability through our own success."

New Leaf Paper builds its environmental mission into the core of its business: its product lines. All New Leaf papers are designed to minimize environmental impact. "Across all the paper we sell, we average over 52 percent postconsumer recycled content," says Mendelsohn. We have twelve product lines with 100 percent recycled content, and where we use virgin wood fiber, we're committed to using sustainably harvested sources. That means our core business serves both our environmental and our financial goals." New Leaf also lessens the amount of toxins going into the soil and water by producing and distributing primarily processed chlorine-free paper. "We offer the broadest selection in North America," the earth-conscious entrepreneur says.

For half of its product lines, New Leaf Paper custom manufactures market-leading environmental papers under the New Leaf brand. For the other half, the company sources existing products that are already environmentally friendly. "Manufacturing paper made from recycled content takes much less energy than creating it from virgin wood," says Mendelsohn. "When we're selling 19,000 tons of paper a year, that translates into enormous benefits in terms of trees, water, and energy saved, and reductions in landfill and CO_2 gas emissions." New Leaf takes pains to be gentler on the planet in smaller ways, too: for its in-house office needs, the company purchases solar- and wind-produced energy.

"It's not enough to put solar panels up while making a product whose process or content is intrinsically harmful to the earth," Mendelsohn points out. "The goal of sustainable businesses should be to eliminate harm and waste completely by building sustainability into the main product."

New Leaf Paper, Recycline, and TS Designs each began life with the express purpose of building a business based on environmentally sound principles. In that sense, they represent exceptions. Most companies start out with other aims in mind. Environmental concerns often enter into the picture much later. For example, at Juniper Communities, a chain of assisted-living facilities, sustainable building standards weren't on the radar screen in the company's early years. Later, when the company chose to adopt those standards when building a new facility, it became clear that doing so didn't just represent a way for the company to demonstrate leadership in its industry and help show the way for other businesses—it probably will in the long run prove to offer a competitive advantage, too, as consumer attitudes continue to evolve toward the expectation that every company must do what's in its power to lessen humanity's impact on the environment.

Juniper Communities
"It Ain't Easy Being Green"

"We built Juniper Village at Chatham, a ninety-five-unit facility, to nationally recognized green building standards," says Lynne Katzmann, president and CEO of Juniper Partners, the parent company of Juniper Communities. "These were the U.S. Green Building Council's Leadership in Energy and Environmental Design [LEED] standards. We believe this is the first and only assisted-living facility in the nation.

"The social impacts are obvious," Katzmann explains. "We have zero storm-water runoff to protect a nearby wetland. We used local construction materials whenever possible. We used materials that emit minimal levels of volatile organic compounds [VOC]. We recycled construction waste. Our building envelope is unique and energy efficient as is our heating, ventilation, and cooling [HVAC] system.

"For example, our HVAC system circulates fresh air rather than recirculating 'bad air' and uses humidifiers to assure the right humidity for our residents and staff. In regard to profits and cost savings, which contribute to profitability, we have nothing to compare it to, but we know we're saving energy. Our lighting system uses energy-efficient bulbs and fixtures and the system itself is timed, meaning lights are automatically off when no one is using the room.

"Environmental sustainability is a clear way to differentiate our product offering in a very competitive market. We market our products and communities under the Green Canopy brand. As our customers become more environmentally and health conscious, it differentiates our offering. We don't charge more, but it attracts more customers. Using paints with low VOC could potentially help with reducing workers' compensation costs, but more practically, it allows us to move patients into [newly painted] odorless rooms more quickly."

Why did Juniper Partners elect to take this initiative? Katzmann explains: "We wanted to create healthy environments for residents, staff, and the communities we're in. It's part of the company's commitment to well-being. We wanted to show a green building could be built cost-efficiently so that we could assure continued affordability for the residents who live there.

"We haven't been able to justify the time and energy to specifically measure our results. That would require baseline information we don't have. However, we continue to use products that meet LEED standards to maintain the community."

It wasn't easy to put this initiative into practice, Katzmann says. The biggest obstacle were "cranky, disinterested architects and contractors. The architects and contractors had to agree to special clauses in their contracts. The LEED standards are very comprehensive and apply to everything from construction waste management, recycling, sourcing locally, etcetera.

"We spent a lot of time and effort educating people on what it meant 'to be green' and begging, pressuring, and coercing them to conform. We had to hold people accountable. We were forcing them to change their behavior in very fundamental ways, and ultimately most wanted to do what was easy rather than what was right. Lip service is free. After the fact, they are glad they did it and are happy to claim the project as theirs. However, in the end, we were not able to get the documentation from them to get [the facility] certified, which was (and still is) a source of great disappointment for us."

The initiative added about 3–4 percent to the company's overall building costs to hire an outside monitoring firm and cover other incremental costs, but the stress on personnel was immeasurable. The project "took a tremendous commitment of energy and personal dedication," notes Katzmann. "We started the project in 1994 and finished in 2001. In addition, we started with a 'brownfield' site, which meant we also went through remediation (to clean up contamination from a prior source) first.

"As Kermit says, 'It ain't easy being green,' but it's well worth it! We're exceptionally proud. In retrospect, I would have worked harder to hire design professionals with prior green building experience. We identified one architectural firm with green experience but did not like their style. We made the decision on aesthetics rather than experience, but now you can get both. I'd still conform to LEED standards again if we had to build a building from the ground up. Also, we now apply the green standards we learned when renovating older buildings in our portfolio." (For more information on the LEED standards, visit the U.S. Green Building Council Web site.)

For Juniper Communities, a newly set policy of adopting sustainable building standards produced great strain on management and a significant shift in business practices. But pursuing environmentally sound policies and practices doesn't always come at great cost in time, money, and stress. A business can take many different steps to start out on the path of sustainability.

Remember the three Rs and one C
Reduce, Reuse, Recycle, and Compost

Almost any business has multiple opportunities to lessen its environmental impact by taking simple, inexpensive steps. Here they are, arranged in descending order of priority, with steps to reduce and reuse materials being most important and recycling being a last resort.

For example, to reduce your use of materials and nonrenewable resources, you might

- Question whether you really need to make a purchase or to travel or whether you can use ground shipment to save energy (and money) as opposed to air shipment

- Conserve heating and cooling energy by adjusting thermostats to 68–70°F in the winter and 74–78°F in the summer

- Turn off lights and computers, and use energy-efficient (Energy Star–rated) computers, appliances, and lighting, including money-saving, long-life, compact fluorescent lightbulbs instead of incandescent bulbs

- Install low-flow toilets and faucet aerators to lessen water use

- Use electronic communication to reduce the amount of printing and paper used

- Consult an architect about salvaging materials and using green design to increase the available natural light in your facilities in order to reduce lighting costs

- Set aside space for secure, sheltered bicycle parking, and offer a stipend to any employee who rides a bike, walks, carpools, or rides public transit to work at least three days per week

- Reduce the amount of packaging used for your products

To reuse materials that might otherwise go to waste, you could

- Redesign your product and packaging so that it can be reused if possible. For example, reuse pallets, utilize reusable totes (shipping containers) and biodegradable peanuts, and ship your goods in cartons you've received from suppliers instead of buying cartons or having your own manufactured

- Seek to place outdated computers, cell phones, and office furniture with schools or nonprofits that can utilize them, and participate in surplus-exchange programs where businesses and government agencies let each other know about unused materials

- Send laser printer cartridges to be refilled with toner and returned to you for reuse

- Use rechargeable batteries that save money and can be reused hundreds of times

- Reuse plates, mugs, and silverware instead of buying disposable plastic plates, cups, and cutlery

- Set up a composting program to take all food scraps to turn them into a great fertilizer, along with any lawn clippings, leaves, and other organic material

To increase the extent to which you recycle the materials you use, you might

- Educate employees on recycling, set recycling goals, and set up a program that makes it easy to recycle and rewards employees for achieving the goals, such as throwing them a party

- Purchase office products (from packaging and furniture to pens and toilet paper) with recycled content in order to close the loop

- Set up a program to recycle all unused electronics (from computers and cell phones) and other products, such as cleaning solvents

- Talk to your municipal government (if it has in place a recycling program) or to a local environmental organization to determine whether you're recycling all the materials that are eligible

- Ask around town to find out whether a local entrepreneur has started a business to pick up materials for recycling

- Insist on the use of at least 30 percent postconsumer recycled paper (paper collected through recycling programs) and nontoxic, agri-based inks in all your printed materials, including publications, letterhead, envelopes, invoices, and other standard business forms

Chances are good that you'll find simple steps such as these to be contagious. Your coworkers may come up with additional ideas—and you may find that the net financial impact is nil, or even positive. Going green may be easier than you think.

Whether you introduce environmentally sound practices into a long-established business or into a newer venture, you will be making an important contribution to improving the quality of our lives. Since we all breathe the air, drink the water, wear clothes, and heat or cool our offices and homes, it's difficult to run a business on the basis of contemporary values without taking energy and resources into account somewhere along the value chain. Still, the environment is just one of the five dimensions of socially responsible business as we've defined the concept. If you've followed us this far, you've surveyed each one of those five dimensions: employees, suppliers, customers, community, and the environment. Now you're ready to join us in a final note, "You Really Can Try This at Home!"

Minimizing Your Environmental Footprint: A Checklist

Here's a list of simple steps you can take to reduce your company's impact on the environment—and demonstrate to your employees, customers, and the general public that your values guide your actions, not just the words you use.

Policy or practice	Adopt?
Consult the list of simple steps to reduce, reuse, and recycle on pages 133—135.	☐
Consult the Social Venture Network's Corporate Standards for Social and Environmental Responsibility and find practices appropriate for your business.	☐
You can't manage it if you don't measure it. Conduct an energy and environmental audit internally, using a third-party auditor, or do what many SVN companies do: have a supplier, customer, or another company audit you in exchange for your auditing it. Perform such audits/assessments periodically so you can monitor your progress.	☐
Find out whether a government agency or a nonprofit organization in your area offers free or low-cost environmental audits. Check out the power company, too, to learn whether it might help you lower your gas and electricity usage.	☐
Based upon the audit's findings, work with your board, partner(s), managers, and employees to draft an environmental policy statement and environmental management system that will guide your company's resource use in the future.	☐
Enlist a member of your staff as a volunteer "environmental coordinator," or, depending on the size of your company, hire a part- or full-time environmental coordinator who will take responsibility for monitoring compliance with your environmental policy statement and canvass other employees for new ideas to lessen the company's environmental impact. Companies that have implemented environmental policies have learned that this position becomes a profit center, not a cost center.	☐
Research the ingredients in your products, including those supplied by vendors, and eliminate all toxic substances.	☐

Policy or practice	Adopt?
Contact your suppliers or vendors to learn about their environmental policies. Switch to new vendors, if necessary, to conform with your expectations that all your suppliers and contractors should minimize their impact on the environment. Place your environmental mission and requirements on your purchase orders.	☐
If you sell products that require replacement, offer your customers an incentive to return the product and packaging to you for reuse when they purchase replacements.	☐
When designing new products and considering the materials to be used in them, plan for the products' full lifetime, including their manufacturing, transportation, use, and disposal. Ensure that your products are either reusable when reconditioned, returnable to you, or readily biodegradable if they can't be recycled.	☐
Before undertaking any major capital project, from building to changing HVAC systems to installing a new piece of equipment, search for existing standards for environmentally superior products (e.g., use the LEED standard) to guide new or renovated building construction, even if you are not seeking LEED certification.	☐
Over time, look at every service you provide and every product you make and ask the question, "Can we do this with sustainable materials, using less material and less energy, and make it less toxic, more durable, refillable, and reusable?"	☐
Whenever possible, use ground versus air transportation and e-mail or fax versus "snail mail."	☐
Investigate whether you can purchase power from renewable sources rather than the dominant power company.	☐
Measure and report cost savings due to reduced energy use and reduced waste.	☐
Explore whether you or your landlord could install solar panels on the roof, energy-efficient lighting, water-efficient fixtures, energy-efficient windows and doors, occupancy sensors, and insulation to lessen or eliminate your purchase of energy.	☐

Minimizing Your Environmental Footprint: A Checklist, *continued*

Policy or practice	Adopt?
Work at making continuous improvement toward minimizing your environmental footprint and maximizing sustainability, no matter how small your progress may seem.	☐

8

You really can try this at home!

It's your turn now.

You've made your way through the seven preceding chapters of this little book (or, at least, we'll humor ourselves with the thought that you haven't cheated by skipping to this point to see how the book ends). You've traveled with us along a path through the five dimensions of a values-driven business, reviewing how you can relate to your employees, your suppliers, your customers, your community, and the environment in mutually beneficial ways. We've described some of the practical steps you can take to live your values—changing the world, making money, and having fun along the way.

Now, don't make the mistake of concluding that we believe any of this is easy. Running a business is anything but easy. Mistakes are inevitable. For example, consider the time that Ben & Jerry's was fined by the local environmental authority for exceeding its waste discharge allotment or when the company ordered too much packaging for one of its flavors and had to dump it or when Mal Warwick & Associates stupidly encouraged a new production manager to take the initiative and ended up spending five years paying off an outrageously inflated printing bill.

Both of us also learned—the hard way—that a values-driven business needs to hire employees who agree with its principles and are motivated by its values. Whenever we hired people who weren't in alignment with who we were, we found that their commitment to the company was limited. Some resented doing socially beneficial acts, seeing them as resulting in extra work and making their jobs harder. They were the exceptions—but each one presented a special challenge.

Ben & Jerry's grew very quickly, and so for a time did Mal Warwick & Associates, adding to the challenge. It's difficult to sustain a corporate culture in the face of rapid growth. Both companies were forced to realize that growth in a values-driven business is sustainable only at the rate at which it's able to train employees and management from within and integrate them into the corporate culture.

No matter your situation, you'll encounter challenges along the way. But if you pursue the path of values-driven business, you'll no doubt find that the rewards vastly outweigh the disadvantages.

To get started, take stock of your situation. Are you feeling fulfilled in your work? Do you wake up in the morning eager for another day on the job? Does your work lend meaning to your life? If not, spend some time considering what really matters in your life. Project yourself twenty years into the future and ask how you'll feel about yourself if you've spent all that time doing what you're doing now. Will you feel as though you've lived a life of purpose and fulfillment? Make a list of your personal values and try matching them against the values that hold sway in your business. Is there a match—or a mismatch?

Values-driven business isn't magical. It's simple, really. All you have to do is live your life and conduct your work in a way that will bring you and the people around you the greatest and deepest satisfaction.

Anybody can do that. Anybody.

And wouldn't the world be a whole lot better off if everybody did?

Resources

Following is a list of Web sites you can visit and organizations you can contact to find information that will help you create a values-driven business.

Avalon Natural Products
(http://www.avalonnaturalproducts.com)

BALLE (Business Alliance for Local Living Economies,
http://www.livingeconomies.org)

BetterWorld Telecom (http://www.betterworldtelecom.com)

Business for Social Responsibility (http://www.bsr.org)

Children's Defense Fund (http://www.childrensdefense.org)

Clif Bar (http://www.clifbar.com)

Co-op America's National Green Pages
(http://www.coopamerica.org/pubs/greenpages)

Eileen Fisher (http://www.eileenfisher.com)

Fenton Communications (http://www.fenton.com)

Give Something Back Business Products
(http://www.givesomethingback.com)

Hewlett-Packard (http://www.hp.com)

Icestone (http://www.icestone.biz)

Immaculate Baking Company
(http://www.immaculatebaking.com)

Investors' Circle (http://www.investorscircle.net)

Juniper Partners (http://juniperpartners.com)

LEED (http://www.usgbc.org/LEED)

Living Wage Resource Center
(http://www.livingwagecampaign.org)

Mal Warwick & Associates (http://www.malwarwick.com)

Natural Step Framework (http://www.naturalstep.org
or http://www.allianceforsustainability.net)

Net Impact (http://www.netimpact.org)

New Leaf Paper (http://www.newleafpaper.com)

Pura Vida Coffee (http://www.puravida.com)

Recycled Paper Printing (http://www.recycledpaper.com)

Recycline (http://www.recycline.com)

Relief Resources (http://www.reliefresources.com)

Seventh Generation (http://www.seventhgeneration.com)

ShoreBank Corporation (http://www.shorebankcorp.com)

ShoreBank Chicago-Detroit (http://www.sbk.com)

ShoreBank Pacific (http://www.eco-bank.com)

Social Venture Network (http://www.svn.org)

TS Designs (http://www.tsdesigns.com)

Vatex America (http://www.vatex.com)

Verité (http://www.verite.org)

Warm Spirit (http://www.warmspirit.com)

White Dog Cafe (http://www.whitedog.com)

Wild Planet (http://www.wildplanet.com)

Working Assets (http://www.workingassets.com)

Worldwise (http://www.worldwise.com)

Notes

1. Marc Olitzsky, Frank L. Schmidt, and Sara L. Rhynes, "Corporate Social and Financial Performance: A Meta-analysis," *Organization Studies* 24 no. 3 (2003): 403–441.

2. Innovest Strategic Value Advisors, "Background," http://www.innovestgroup.com/background_1.htm (accessed December 17, 2005).

3. Mathis Wackernagel and William E. Rees, *Our Ecological Footprint: Reducing Human Impact on the Earth* (Gabriola Island, BC: New Society Publishers, 1996).

4. Paul Hawken, e-mail message to author, December 15, 2005.

5. World Commission on Environment and Development, *Our Common Future* (Oxford: Oxford University Press, 1987).

Index

About Social Venture Network

SVN transforms the way the world does business by connecting, leveraging, and promoting a global community of leaders for a more just and sustainable economy.

Since its founding in 1987, SVN has grown from a handful of visionary individuals into a vibrant community of 400 business owners, investors, and nonprofit leaders who are advancing the movement for social responsibility in business. SVN members believe in a new bottom line for business, one that values healthy communities and the human spirit as well as high returns.

As a network, SVN facilitates partnerships, strategic alliances, and other ventures that promote social and economic justice. SVN compiles and promotes best practices for socially responsible enterprises and produces unique conferences that support the professional and personal development of business leaders and social entrepreneurs.

Please visit http://www.svn.org for more information on SVN membership, initiatives, and events.

About the Authors

Ben Cohen is a cofounder of Ben & Jerry's. The business started in 1978 as a homemade-ice-cream parlor in a former gas station on an investment of $8,000. In 1988, Ben & Jerry's was named U.S. Small Business of the Year by President Ronald Reagan. The company also received the Corporate Giving Award from the Council on Economic Priorities, presented by Joanne Woodward at a reception in New York City, for donating 7.5 percent of its pretax income to nonprofit organizations through the Ben & Jerry's Foundation. By 1999, the enterprise had an annual sales volume of over $250 million with 700 employees, and Ben had become a pioneer in the area of socially responsible business. Despite Ben's efforts to keep the company independent, Ben & Jerry's was acquired by Unilever in 2000.

Today, Ben is president of Business Leaders for Sensible Priorities and TrueMajority.org. BLSP is a group of 1,000 business leaders working to fund social needs at no additional taxpayer expense by transferring money from outmoded cold war–era military expenditures. TrueMajority.org monitors Congress on issues of social justice, environmental sustainability, and international cooperation. When constituents' voices count, the organization's 500,000 members receive an e-alert. With one click, they send a fax to their congresspeople.

Mal Warwick has been active in promoting social and environmental responsibility in the business community nationwide for more than a decade. He was a cofounder of Business for Social Responsibility and served on its board during its inaugural year.

In 2001, after more than a decade as an active member, he was elected to the board of Social Venture Network and served as chair (2002–2006). He also served on the Founding Advisory Board of the Center for Responsible Business at the Haas School of Business at the University of California, Berkeley, in 2002–2003.

As a consultant, author, and public speaker, Mal has been involved in the not-for-profit sector for more than forty years. He is the founder and chairman of Mal Warwick & Associates, a fund-raising and marketing agency that has served nonprofit organizations since 1979, and founded or cofounded three other companies that provide fund-raising services to nonprofit organizations throughout the country. He has written, coauthored, or edited seventeen previous books, including the standard fund-raising texts, *Revolution in the Mailbox* and *How to Write Successful Fundraising Letters*. Mal is a popular speaker and workshop leader at gatherings of fundraisers throughout the world. He has taught fund-raising on six continents to nonprofit leaders from more than 100 countries.

Other Titles in the Social Venture Network Series

True to Yourself: Leading a Values-Based Business
by Mark Albion
This is an engaging, accessible guide to a critical component of socially responsible business: effective leadership. Mark Albion, author of the *New York Times* bestseller *Making a Life, Making a Living,* argues that small-business leaders concerned with more than the bottom line are not only more fulfilled but also more successful with more sustainable lives. He uses real-world examples to identify the qualities and specific practices of small-business leaders who combine profit with purpose, margin with mission, value with values. Whether you're just starting out or many years on your way, *True to Yourself* will help you to get and stay on track.
July 2006, $12.00, paperback, ISBN 978-1-57675-378-1 or 1-57675-378-6

Marketing That Matters: 10 Practices to Drive
Your Socially Responsible Business
by Chip Conley and Eric Friedenwald-Fishman
"Marketing" is not a dirty word or a last resort—it is key to advancing the mission of any socially responsible business. In this book, award-winning marketers Chip Conley and Eric Friedenwald-Fishman offer values-driven businesspeople an in-the-trenches guide to building an effective marketing model for their companies. For overworked entrepreneurs who want to match their mission with their values but lack the time or the training to develop a strategy from scratch, this field manual provides practical steps for incorporating marketing as a core element of the business. Full of inspiring stories, key concepts, and tested advice, this book shows how to sell what you do without selling your soul.
October 2006, $12.00, paperback, ISBN 978-1-57675-383-5 or
1-57675-383-2

Growing Local Value: How to Build a Values-Driven Business That Strengthens Your Community
by Laury Hammel and Gun Denhart

This down-to-earth guide explains how to build or expand a values-driven business that is deeply embedded in the life of the local community. While most people think of "community engagement" only in terms of philanthropy or volunteerism, entrepreneurs Laury Hammel and Gun Denhart show how every aspect of a business (from product creation to employee recruitment to vendor selection to raising capital) holds the dual promise of bigger profits and a stronger local community. Including such practical tools as a Community Involvement Self-Assessment, *Growing Local Value* explores the full spectrum of ways in which a business can contribute to its community—and the benefits it receives when it does.

November 2006, $12.00, paperback, ISBN 978-1-57675-371-2 or 1-57675-371-9

For more information, check out the Social Venture Network Series Web page: www.svnbooks.com.

About Berrett-Koehler Publishers

Berrett-Koehler is an independent publisher dedicated to an ambitious mission: Creating a World that Works for All.

We believe that to truly create a better world, action is needed at all levels—individual, organizational, and societal. At the individual level, our publications help people align their lives and work with their deepest values. At the organizational level, our publications promote progressive leadership and management practices, socially responsible approaches to business, and humane and effective organizations. At the societal level, our publications advance social and economic justice, shared prosperity, sustainable development, and new solutions to national and global issues.

We publish groundbreaking books focused on each of these levels. To further advance our commitment to positive change at the societal level, we have recently expanded our line of books in this area and are calling this expanded line "BK Currents."

A major theme of our publications is "Opening Up New Space." They challenge conventional thinking, introduce new points of view, and offer new alternatives for change. Their common quest is changing the underlying beliefs, mindsets, institutions, and structures that keep generating the same cycles of problems, no matter who our leaders are or what improvement programs we adopt.

We strive to practice what we preach—to operate our publishing company in line with the ideas in our books. At the core of our approach is stewardship, which we define as a deep sense of responsibility to administer the company for the benefit of all of our "stakeholder" groups: authors, customers, employees, investors, service providers, and the communities and environment around us. We seek to establish a partnering relationship with each stakeholder that is open, equitable, and collaborative.

We are gratified that thousands of readers, authors, and other friends of the company consider themselves to be part of the "BK Community." We hope that you, too, will join our community and connect with us through the ways described on our website at www.bkconnection.com.

Be Connected

Visit Our Website

Go to www.bkconnection.com to read exclusive previews and excerpts of new books, find detailed information on all Berrett-Koehler titles and authors, browse subject-area libraries of books, and get special discounts.

Subscribe to Our Free E-Newsletter

Be the first to hear about new publications, special discount offers, exclusive articles, news about bestsellers, and more! Get on the list for our free e-newsletter by going to www.bkconnection.com.

Participate in the Discussion

To see what others are saying about our books and post your own thoughts, check out our blogs at www.bkblogs.com.

Get Quantity Discounts

Berrett-Koehler books are available at quantity discounts for orders of ten or more copies. Please call us toll-free at (800) 929-2929 or email us at bkp.orders@aidcvt.com.

Host a Reading Group

For tips on how to form and carry on a book reading group in your workplace or community, see our website at www.bkconnection.com.

Join the BK Community

Thousands of readers of our books have become part of the "BK Community" by participating in events featuring our authors, reviewing draft manuscripts of forthcoming books, spreading the word about their favorite books, and supporting our publishing program in other ways. If you would like to join the BK Community, please contact us at bkcommunity@bkpub.com.